HARDSHIP ALASKA

DONALD PROFFIT

Epicenter Press Inc.
Alaska Book Adventures™

Kenmore, WA

Epicenter Press Inc.
Alaska Book Adventures™

6524 NE 181st St., Suite 2, Kenmore, WA 98028

Epicenter Press is a regional press publishing nonfiction
books about the arts, history, environment, and diverse
cultures and lifestyles of Alaska and the Pacific Northwest.
For more information, visit www.EpicenterPress.com

Hardship Alaska
Copyright © 2023 by Donald Proffit

Cover design: Scott Book
Interior design: Melissa Vail Coffman

ISBN: 978-1-684920-57-0 (Trade Paperback)
ISBN: 978-1-684920-58-7 (Ebook)

Library of Congress Control Number: 2022936036

Produced in the United States of America

In line at lunch I cross my fork and spoon
to ward off complicity—the ordered life
our leaders have offered us. Thin as a knife,
our chance to live depends on such a sign
while others talk and The Pentagon from the moon
is bouncing exact commands: "Forget your faith;
be ready for whatever it takes to win: we face
annihilation unless all citizens get in line."

I bow and cross my fork and spoon: somewhere
other citizens more fearfully bow
in a place terrorized by their kind of oppressive state.
Our signs both mean, "You hostages over there
will never be slaughtered by my act." Our vows
cross: never to kill and call it fate.

—William Stafford, *Objector*

Contents

Preface

THIS BOOK BEGAN AS A COLLECTION of vignettes written while on airplanes over the last fifteen years or so, each one written in the time it would take to fly from point A to point B. It was a way to remember people and places I had come to know while a conscientious objector during the Vietnam War. These memories had been captured in photographs, each snapshot a sacred object to hold and gaze upon during the ritual of remembering. The photos, soiled and scarred by a Delaware River flood, now lie decomposing in some landfill in New Jersey. They had lacked scuppers to divert the muddied water toward lesser valued mementos trapped in the basement. With the loss of these photos, writing then became a way to remember, a way to hold on to these images as they gradually wash away from my memory.

The vignettes have now transformed into chapters and sketchy recall has led to more hours of research than I thought my patience could handle. The process of writing has helped me recreate what took place not only in each photo, but also immediately before and after, providing a defensive wall against the distortion that can seep into memory, altering time, place, and experience.

A few of these memories continue to haunt me as often do an unresolved conversation or parting over dinner or by a front door, in bed or at a bar. Others, however, have been exorcized completely of any lingering ghosts, leaving me with a better understanding of who I was during that time and who I am today.

I've attempted to contact the people in this book for permission to use their names; however, with fifty years gone since these events took place, many are no longer with us. Their names, however, are, and as they are portrayed in good light within these pages, their names remain unchanged. For others, those who joined me in indelicate acts of discovering who we are when we were young and for those whose names I can no longer recall or the few I could not locate, I've given fictitious names. I've also given names to the occasional Samaritans, even though we never exchanged names or formally met, who guided and protected me along this journey, those who appear as if by magic in a time of need and then vanish—the brief and intimate encounters with angelic strangers.

Foretellings

As a kid I would paint watercolors of mountains I had never seen. I spent hours brushing gray wash backgrounds suitable for both sky and rocky terrain. Clouds sweeping up from the base of the range, pushed aloft by winds cutting across the valley and coming to rest, as if asleep, on the tops of mountains.

* * *

I wrote a poem in college, I think it came from a dream, of men selling salmon, frozen, block-cut and wrapped in brown paper, which I bought. They stood at the end of a road beneath a bluff, a boat ramp of sorts, against a bleak horizon of a cold bay. Large chunks of ice sat still in the water with no place to go. Across the inlet slept a giant that resembled a mountain.

The Lottery

"**H**EY, ARE WE READY TO DO THIS TONIGHT?"
I met up with Herbie, my former college roommate when I had lived on campus before taking a job as dorm proctor, occasional bus driver and gym teacher at a small, boys boarding school. I had just made my way over to Westminster Choir College, where we were both seniors, to meet with Herbie for supper.

"Good to see you. Yeah, I'm ready. How about The Annex?"

Herb and I left the campus turning right onto Hamilton Street until it became Wiggins. We came to Princeton Cemetery, which always made me think of my first gin and *Wink*. It was offered by an upperclassman who lived off campus on Madison Street. Loopy after consuming more of the grapefruit flavored potion than I should have, I somehow got turned around as I made my way back to campus and ended up in the cemetery at Aaron Burrs' grave. Somebody on the sidewalk called out, it must have been another Choir College student.

"Westminster's this way," he said, and I followed him home.

Once Herb and I got to the cemetery, we turned left onto Tulane, and zig-zagged our way through the alley until we reached 128½

Nassau. Across the street stood Firestone Library and beyond it, the University Chapel where we'd graduate the next spring. Walking along Princeton sidewalks, especially at the beginning of the academic year as leaves changed from green to rust along with the accompanying smell of decaying vegetation, always made me feel collegiate. Even on this early December evening, with the temperature stuck in the mid-30°s and leaves long fallen from the trees, the feeling lingered.

We pulled the door open and descended the flight of stairs into the sheltered warmth of The Annex, a popular subterranean restaurant frequented by Princeton students, academics, and locals. It was also a place where discrete Westminster male students could temporarily become ivy leaguers, if only for a few hours while eating a reasonably priced, big-portioned meal in the dark oak wainscoted dining room, or maybe having a burger and a few beers in the more intimate bar. Adding to the restaurant's atmosphere was a collection of Princeton University football team photographs, crossed oars, and related gear chronicling decades of athletic combat. Unlike modern-day sports bars where pirated memorabilia from local high schools, colleges or nearby professional teams are strewn across the walls and dangled from the rafters like decoys to ensnare customers, The Annex's decor was authentic, not some artificial ploy to fill tables, but rather a deliberate show of pride and unmasked loyalty to the university across the street.

"Let's eat in the bar tonight," Herb suggested. The bar had a different vibe from the dining room—cozier with a fratty touch. I nodded in agreement, and we made our way into the back room.

We grabbed a table, ordered a couple of beers and burgers. Tonight, the place seemed more populated with Princeton students than was typical for a Monday night. A handful of Tigers came over to our table.

"Boys," one of the men addressed us, "do you mind if we join you?"

Herb and I were at a table that could snuggly hold six, and as the bar was quickly filling up, we looked at each other to make sure we agreed.

"Sure, I think we can make this work. Please have a seat." We did a round of introductions over a round of beers.

It was a rare occasion to have University and Choir College men in such close proximity to each other. Princeton men tended to keep their distance from us, as there was a sustained rumor that most men from Westminster were *queers*, which may or may not have been true. I remember sitting at the very same table with four or five other Westminster students a year or so earlier. Someone at the table had gotten a hold of a copy of *Bob Damron's Address Book*, a pocket-sized compendium of purported gay bars, bathhouses, highway rest stops and other unsavory haunts that catered to or were frequented by homosexuals at a time when socializing as a gay person meant going underground to stay safe. It even included AYOR warnings—AT YOUR OWN RISK—for those places and areas where police could be watching, or unsavory types might be lurking in the shadows to cause you harm or worse. To our surprise, he had read that The Annex was listed as a non-AYOR establishment where homosexuals might be present. With that newly discovered information, we increased our visits from the occasional to weekly for food and drink. We had a mission. We became regulars and took up residence at one of the large round tables in the bar, always waiting to spot someone like us, as we had read in the *Address Book*. This went on for a while, never seeing anyone who might be gay until one evening we realized, and were slightly disappointed to learn, that we were the very homosexuals that we were looking for and that most likely generated the listing in the guidebook. Our weekly visits dropped off after we came to that realization.

On this night, however, there were no barriers between us and the Princeton students. No worries that we might flirt with one of the boys and be ridiculed for it. Rumors and differences no longer seemed important. What mattered tonight was that the first draft lottery in nearly three decades would determine who among us of a certain age would be the first to be called up to the US military by the Selective Service. I can't remember whether we watched the broadcast on a small black and white television set up on the bar, CBS News was airing the event live from the Selective Service headquarters in Washington, or on a portable radio tuned to the university's student run FM station, WPRB. Either way, we sat together, drank beer, and listened intently as the birth dates of all US males aged nineteen to twenty-six, were randomly drawn. Each date had been printed on an individual slip of paper, rolled tight and placed in its own blue plastic capsule and casually tossed in an extra-large glass container that resembled a 10-gallon cylindrical aquarium. As each capsule was drawn, opened and the date read aloud, it was assigned a number in sequence from 1 to 366, and slipped into a corresponding slot on a large display board. A New York Congressman, Alexander Pirnie, dug deep into the jar and drew the first date, September 14. It was assigned 001. Because President Nixon wanted to have draft-age men involved in the process for transparency's sake, the remaining capsules were drawn by members of the Selective Service Youth Advisory Council, which to me seemed inappropriate. I didn't quite see them as traitors, but nevertheless didn't want somebody our age having my fate in their hands, even if it was just for show. Maybe it was a tactic to shift blame, should you get a low number, onto someone less blameworthy rather than an elected official. This was not a lottery that you wanted to win, not when the grand prize included an all-inclusive two-year tour of duty slogging through Vietnamese jungles and facing possible death in a war that made no sense to me.

Once delegates from the Selective Service Youth Advisory Council took over, instead of picking one capsule at a time, they began to grab five or six at once. Based on predictions by the Selective Service, we already assumed that if your birthday fell in the first third of the dates drawn, you'd be assigned a number between 1-122, and it would certainly guarantee that you'd be drafted and more than likely face combat in Vietnam. The next third of the dates drawn received numbers between 123-244 and would face a fifty-fifty chance of being called up for service, and the last third, 245-366, would never be drafted at all.

One of the Princeton boys bought another round of beers for the table as the sequence of assigned numbers climbed into the fifties. I was still grabbing bites of my burger between talk of war, politics, campus life and birthdays when it happened. The rolled piece of paper holding my birthdate, January 19, was pulled from its hiding place among the hundreds of others waiting in the cylindrical glass container. Callous fingers dug into the blue plastic cocoon and unfurled the note, a butterfly not yet ready to emerge. It was then passed on to someone I imagined to be an evil lepidopterist, who indelicately pinned the date to a mounting board and cataloged it as specimen Number 58.

Time stopped. I looked over at Herbie, both of us realizing that at that moment everything had changed for me, for us, and would never be the same. Those around the table put down their mugs of beer, burgers, and fries, all of us strangers until tonight, and looked at me with sympathetic eyes, the first at the table to be called.

"I'm so sorry, Buzzy," Herbie was the first to speak. The rest at the table took turns offering their condolences to me.

It was all I could do to remain with my group at The Annex after my number was assigned. I had immediately lost my appetite and pushed my plate away. Out of loyalty to those around me, who'd invested their time, talk and table camaraderie, I stayed and had another beer and waited to see how the numbers played out for the rest of us. It would be a long night. Herbie, December 12, drew 314.

What was I going to do? I knew in my heart that I was incapable of killing another person should I be drafted and sent off to war. I wasn't someone who ever thought of causing harm to any living thing for that matter, even those who had harmed me. And while

I felt this all deeply and instinctively knew it was who I was, I had never fully articulated it before to myself or anyone else. Somehow, I knew at that moment that I would have to bring clarity to what I assumed were my core beliefs. It was as if I was a potter sitting at his wheel, centering a lump of clay and shaping what I believed and valued in my heart into a vessel that I could show to others so that they could see who I truly was.

Duty Calls

"HOW IS IT YOU CLAIM TO BE A CONSCIENTIOUS OBJECTOR, a pacifist in all accounts, yet you engage in a display of violence on stage? You're even wounded." He pointed at my broken arm which I had gotten in rehearsal during a fight sequence. "Are you not a man of your convictions? Perhaps you should've sat that scene out like you want to do with this war."

He nodded to the board's executive secretary, Mamie, who dismissed me with a curt flick of her wrist.

"Thank you, Mr. Proffit, that will be all. You'll hear from us soon."

Stunned, I left the room and ran down the flight of stairs past a full-blown bingo game taking place in the main assembly room of the Allentown chapter of the Independent Order of Odd Fellows and out onto the still hot city sidewalk on North Ninth Street. I was so angry and distraught that I had trouble catching my breath, the heat and humidity didn't make it any easier. What just happened? Could it be that even with the letters of support from my parents, college chaplain, Jewish and Christian leaders, and friends, that being a chorus boy in a musical play did me in?

* * *

MY REQUEST TO APPEAL MY 1-A CLASSIFICATION had been set for 7:00 p.m. on July 20, 1970. Like prepping for a role in a play, I needed to know my lines cold and be able to make an impact on my audience, my local draft board. But I also needed to remember, and remember well, that this was not a play I was rehearsing; it was war, and the stakes were decidedly higher, and the outcome could be far worse than being panned in the local newspaper weekend entertainment section.

Days before my hearing I had requested a meeting with a Government Appeal Agent to go over my case. I needed to get this right. The outcome of that night's hearing would determine whether I'd be granted conscientious objector status or must take my appeal to the next level. If I ran out of appeals, would I be facing jail time for refusing to carry a gun? I had never held a gun before or had any desire to hold one ever, not even for sport. Would I then need to escape to Canada? I needed to stay calm and focus on what mattered most right now, being prepared for when I'd meet with my draft board.

The meeting with the agent was set for 9:00 a.m. the morning of my hearing. Its purpose was to provide advice and assistance, within reason, and to have an opportunity to review the contents of my Selective Service file. The agent would not be present during my hearing that evening, that was not his responsibility, He was not my defender. I'd be on my own.

I drove to the Odd Fellows Building on North Ninth, a fraternal order with a mission to "visit the sick, relieve the distressed, bury the dead and educate the orphan," oh, and rent space to the local draft board. I learned later, when I returned that night, that bingo also played a big part in relieving the distressed, or so it seemed.

The morning meeting felt productive and the Government Appeal Agent, Joseph Rosenfeld, was helpful in answering my questions, but he sat quietly beside me sipping coffee from a paper cup, watching me carefully as I rifled through the items in my file. I couldn't add or remove anything—the letters of support, which were the key items I wanted to make sure were there; the results of the draft physical from months before, which I passed with flying red, white and blue colors, even though I passed out between the siphoning of a vial or two of my blood and then having my blood pressure taken at the very next check point. When I came to, I discovered myself strapped to a gurney, a muscular sergeant slapping my face. I think I even emitted a soft moan as I opened my eyes, maybe a bit turned on by the uniformed man standing over me. As soon as I could state my name and age, what day it was and the name of the president, he unstrapped me and escorted me right back in line where I was handed off to a medic holding a blood pressure cuff. My blood pressure had dropped significantly, but no matter, my examiners determined me to be in tip-top shape.

The file also held the running record of my student deferments from when I turned eighteen in high school and over four years of college. I felt like I was seeing my life the way the Selective Service saw me, only defined by the contents of my file, limited to my student deferment classifications, 1-S, when in high school and four years as 2-S, during college. There was also my recent 1-A status indicating that I was available immediately for military service, but not the 1-O classification that I needed; the one that stated I was assigned into the conscientious objector work program and ordered to complete 24 consecutive months of civilian alternative service with an approved agency or organization—the same amount of time as someone conscripted into the army. The approved service had to demonstrate that the CO was meaningfully contributing to the "maintenance of the national health, safety, and interest" of the nation.

It was all so cut and dry, lacking any warmth, except for the letters of support from my parents, friends, college officials and the diverse assortment of religious types, my college chaplain, and supervisors at the Jewish day camp where I had served as a camp counselor that summer. But were the contents of my file enough to show the board who I was? Would I be able to prove to them during my in-person appeal later that night, that I was a pacifist, that I couldn't do what they were asking me to do, that it could lead to my exile, imprisonment or death? Over the months that had gone by since December 1, 1969, when I drew number 58 in the draft lottery, I had reached clarity on what I believed and valued regarding war and my unwillingness to participate in any form of it.

At 7:00 p.m. sharp I was ushered into a room on the second floor, a room no longer used by the Odd Fellows, but instead leased to the Selective Service and now functioning as the hearing room for my appeal. Members of the draft board sat side by side at a long folding table, the kind you'd see at a church potluck social. The chairman sat in the middle chair flanked on either side by his fellow board members, all men, all white. The only woman in the room was Mamie Bramwell, the board's executive secretary.

I was prepared. I delivered my remarks with only the occasional stutter until I found my ground.

"Good evening, gentlemen. My Name is Donald Lyle Proffit, Jr., Selective Service number 36-89-48-39. Thank you for allowing me to speak with you about my request to be classified as a conscientious objector.

"My file contains letters of support from people who know and love me. People who know what I believe and what I stand for.

"I've just completed four years of college where I've trained to be a teacher. During that time, I've also worked with children in schools and most recently right here in Allentown at the Jewish Community Center's summer day camp.

"I work with children and plan on doing that for the rest of my life. I want to serve this country, but I'm asking that you permit me to do this in a manner that best uses my talents and abilities. I was not raised to inflict pain on another human being, and I know in my heart, that I'm incapable of killing another whether in times of peace or war. There is no justification that I can see in the act of killing or serving in a manner that may lead to the death of another, especially a child . . ."

My remarks stressed my work with children and teaching, my humanism, avoiding any mention of religious beliefs that could qualify me for exemption, because I didn't have any defined or that could be defended, except for what I was taught by my mother as a child. She had told me that we each carried a piece of God within us, a spark of the divine, and that heaven and hell, but mostly hell, only existed in the here and now, our good days and bad, happy times or sad—not some magical realm inhabiting the space above or below us. There was a point, however, when my mother on a morphine drip and strapped to an ICU bed following a serious traffic accident, believed that the Berkshires was heaven. Whenever I would visit her in the hospital, she'd ask me if I also saw dead people standing around her, her mother and departed relatives moving about pine trees in a gentle snow fall.

To be safe, within a few weeks of being born, my parents had me christened in the Congregational Church across from the town hall, on the edge of the village commons in the town of Lunenburg Massachusetts just in case they were wrong and those two places, heaven and hell, existed. But for most of my life, I was merely a dilettante when it came to the visible church, an amused dabbler in the pomp and circumstance of it all, the theatrics, vestments, music, and processions. I was a moveable feast never staying too long at any one table, unless of course I found my way into or was asked to join the choir or contribute in other artistic ways like liturgical dance (I danced a butch Adam one Christmas Eve at the Presbyterian Church in Bethlehem as part of a service of lessons and carols), then I'd take my seat and eat.

One other thing, one teaching, did stay with me throughout my life and no doubt was influenced by these early religious explorations—"Do unto others as you would have them do unto you." The "love thy neighbor" commandment meant something to me. I had never been in a fight or physically lashed out at anyone. This pacifist's take on my interaction with others influenced my opposition to war. I used it in my defense.

Besides my prepared remarks, I only carried one other piece of paper into my hearing that night, a note containing a quotation by Mahatma Gandhi. I had been given the words, typed on a torn-out sheet of steno pad paper by the Princeton University draft counselor I met with two months earlier in May. As he and I sat in a small, borrowed room in Nassau Hall, he gave me the basics on becoming a conscientious objector, stressing the importance of declaring my opposition to all war, not the one war we were all consumed with at the time. He also stressed how, because I hadn't declared my conscientious objector status at the time I enrolled in the draft on my eighteenth birthday, that doing so now would be difficult. The fact that I had already had my initial induction physical along with a draft lottery number of fifty-eight also added to my dilemma and brought me closer to what I feared most at the time—having to go to war and not being able to survive because of my pacifism. Based on our conversation, he suggested that the Gandhi quote would help me better define my stand. He had given it to me to stress the difference between a conscientious objector who was opposed to any military involvement whatsoever and a conscientious objector not opposed to serving in the military in a non-combatant role, like being an orderly in a field hospital, emptying bedpans and cleaning wounds, close to the action but not necessarily part of it. I had decided that the latter was not an option for me. If I was involved in the machinery of war, even as the tiniest cog, I'd consider myself just as culpable, a willing participant to someone else's death. Gandhi's words made sense to me, clarified what I believed but could not articulate at the time. I had the quote with me for support that night, should the board suggest that I serve in a noncombatant role in the military. The quote read, "I make no distinction, from the point of view of ahimsa between combatants and non-combatants. He who volunteers to serve a band of dacoits, by working as their carrier, or their watchman while they are about their business, or their nurse when they are wounded, is as much guilty of dacoity as the dacoits themselves. In the same way those who confine themselves to attending to the wounded in battle cannot be absolved from the guilt of war." I didn't need to read it during my hearing, the subject of which kind of conscientious objector I might be never came up. I still have that quote hammered out on a portable typewriter by the Princeton student, its misaligned typeface resembling the notes of a simple melody inked on manuscript paper.

The appeal seemed to be going well until the very end when one board member eyed the cast on my arm and leaned over to whisper something to the chairman. I had broken it during a rehearsal, a local summer stock production of *Man of La Mancha*. I played one of the muleteers. I loved being in these performances, whether in summer stock or community theater at other times of the year. It was my safe place where I felt welcomed and accepted. It fed my passion for the arts, its multidisciplinary approach allowing me to sing, dance and act along with building and painting sets. It defined who I was at the time, and I felt part of a caring family who understood and accepted each other.

The production was part of Guthsville Playhouse's summer season. The theater, an old leaky, bat-infested barn behind a Pennsylvania fieldstone-clad hotel in the tiny village of the same name just north of Allentown, had burned to the ground that May. The only good thing about the fire was we would no longer have to endure the stench of rendered horse meat drifting from the ALPO dog food processing plant directly across the highway where old horses and the occasional mule casually grazed, long since written off as losses from whatever farm they had come. The factory sat atop a slight hill as the animals waited patiently in a fenced field below until it was their time to be processed. The idyllic pasture nothing more than a death row cellblock for these used beasts.

The building sat in indifference at the edge of the road while its stench stretched across the highway and smothered our performances each night. Especially on humid summer nights when the odor would settle inside the barn on rows of seats and sections of scenery, in costumes and wigs, causing audience and actors alike to gag; the flutter of playbills and bats' wings doing little to fan away the fetid air. Now with the barn destroyed and no place to perform, the Playhouse took up residence five miles south in Dorney Park's fabled Castle Garden, a massive wooden pavilion built back in the time of dance marathons and flapperdom.

I explained my broken left arm to the board after I'd seen a couple members staring at my cast, which ran from my elbow to my wrist. I told them how I fractured it in rehearsal during the opening scene of the popular Don Quixote-inspired musical, *The Man of La Mancha*. There's a struggle, a fight in the prison's common room, a dudgeon where the accused awaited trial during the Spanish Inquisition. Cervantes had just been escorted down an immense staircase that lowers to the stage floor on heavy iron chains from high above upstage center, and we, the accused, on seeing him, restrain him and fight over his possessions. Something was off during that rehearsal. Crossing my wrists, I demonstrated how my arm got broken when a fellow actor missed his blocking and accidentally fell, full force to the stage floor, pinning me beneath him and shattering my wrist. I was about to tell the board how to buy tickets for this stellar production when the man directing my inquisition, the draft board chairman, suddenly looked up from my file, one eyebrow cocked in feigned alarm. He began questioning why I was seeking a conscientious objector classification from the draft board when clearly, according to him, there was no way I could be deserving of the classification if I engaged in stage combat in a play.

And that was the moment I realized the board's chair was questioning my integrity, drawing what I felt was an unfair comparison between my pacifism and performing in summer stock. I could survive *Man of La Mancha* with a broken arm and go on living, but not necessarily a war. This was not at all how I imagined the evening would play out. I was certain, maybe naively so, that I'd walk away with a more positive outcome, some promising gesture, a smile, a nod or confirming wink, that a 1-O reclassification would be delivered to my mailbox within two weeks.

Following my unsuccessful July 20 hearing, I remembered what the government appeal agent had told me should the local board once again deny my request. He said I could then reach out to the state Selective Service appeal board. It would be my last chance for an appeal, apart from appealing directly to the President through the national appeal board. I appealed to the state board and was denied. I then submitted my last appeal to the national board and waited. I held little hope for a positive resolution from the national board. Based on all that had so far transpired regarding my ability to convince the Selective Service of my pacifism that summer, I was now resigned to reconsider my last two options—federal prison for five years or escaping to Canada. Both held unknown futures. Five years in confinement seemed unfathomable to me. The criminal record alone would prevent me from ever teaching, something that I had trained so hard for during college. Who knew what five years in jail might do to me, mentally and physically? Of the two unknowns, seeking exile in Canada at least seemed to hold the possibility to lead a normal life. At least my parents could cross the border for a visit now and then.

Time was up. I needed to choose one. I went to the desk in my bedroom and dug through my papers until I found the Canadian immigration application I had already filled out, except for one remaining item at the end of the form. Just one line remained blank. I grabbed a pen and signed my name.

Options

M Y OPTIONS AT THIS POINT WERE extremely limited and my Selective Service lottery number, drawn the previous December, was fifty-eight, a guarantee that my induction would be on the fast track once I graduated Westminster in May. I had already endured the nightmarish draft physical earlier that spring, when young men looking like lost boys boarded a caravan of buses idling in front of the Trenton train station and were transported north along the New Jersey Turnpike to the military induction center in downtown Newark.

Stripped to my underwear and directed to remain silent, my clothes placed in a small wire basket and slotted into walled shelves with a hundred more, I joined the naked and bewildered in single-file formation as we were pushed through an obstacle course of health checks, bloodletting, and mental screenings. Those that questioned, spoke out or otherwise failed to follow the drill, were culled from our group, escorted to an empty hallway or stairwell, and provided with a toothbrush for scrubbing the wall and floor tiles. We would occasionally see them on their hands and knees scouring away when we'd pass a doorway which looked out into the hallway. I think it was a setup, a *tableau vivant*—a staged warning to the rest of us: you did what you were told or else.

* * *

I HAD TRAINING FOR THIS AS A CHILD, rehearsals for this very moment. In elementary school one could not escape the Salk polio vaccine inoculations performed with Fritz Lang-inspired mechanical glass and metal syringes on small weak arms. I tried once, in a panic, but was forcibly moved from my place at the end of the line to the very front by one, who, a few minutes earlier, was a benevolent and compassionate teacher now turned strategic staff sergeant. All very public in the school cafeteria.

And then, the nasty tasting fluoride treatment with diabolical clamps and stiff, saliva-sucking cotton dowels squeezed into tiny mouths, all while seated in a portable dentist's chair, ceremoniously placed, yet again, in the cafeteria as classmates watched in horror as they awaited their turn. No wonder I had trouble eating at school, or in any public setting for years after.

But then, the ultimate terror, the sixth-grade school physical as you were funneled into a recessed corner of the nurse's office, shielded by a rickety trifold screen offering little privacy as the doctor (I think it was a doctor) shouted every ugly detail about your physical shortcomings to the nurse as she filled in your chart on the other side of the divider. The rest of the boys waited uncomfortably in a line, listening to each tattled malady, and watching the nurse's sometimes shaming expressions as she gleefully wrote down the diagnosis.

"Enlarged breasts!"

I remember the terror of having to face a gauntlet of twelve-year-old boys, eyes staring, as I quickly dressed and coming out from behind the screen, made my way back to the classroom in shame.

I felt the same way now, fighting the urge to raise my arms and cover my chest as I stood alongside three others in front of a

gridded backdrop indicating height in feet and inches as two uniformed men decided on and called out your body shape, holding
clipboards and pens, making notes on our appearances as if we
were on an auction block. The men called out their findings. One of
my line buddies was an ectomorph, tall and lean, the other one was
rounder, an endomorph. I ended up with mesomorph. I looked up
the term once I got back to college that evening and smiled.

* * *

I FELT SAD AND ANGRY AFTER THE KENT STATE KILLINGS which
added to my concern about my own situation of having drawn a
low draft lottery number, 58. I'd be drafted as soon as I graduated
unless something changed in my favor, an occupational deferment
if I found a teaching job for the fall. I decided to seek draft counseling from a student volunteer at Princeton University who strongly
suggested I go to Philadelphia to meet with someone at the CCCO,
the Central Committee for Conscientious Objectors.

Talking with CCCO staff in Philadelphia and reading a half
dozen pamphlets detailing the rules, restrictions, and an individual's rights in time of war, I determined that my options were
limited to four. I could file for CO status and hope I get it. One
drawback the CCCO counselor told me was that because I hadn't
declared pacifism or provided reason for being a conscientious
objector when I registered for the draft at eighteen, it would be
more difficult to persuade my local draft board of that fact now. I
had already had to deal with my local board on a couple occasions
when I didn't receive my student deferment for an academic year,
including the fact that I was called up for a draft physical while still
classified 2-S.

I'm not sure I even knew what my options were with respect to
claiming to be a conscientious objector in 1966 as a high school
senior. My parents and I never discussed the possibility. When
I turned eighteen, I registered for the draft as the law stipulated.

There was no discussion about what that meant or if there were any options I should've known about. It was what young men did and what my parents expected me to do, too. If I knew that my opposition to war or serving in the armed forces as a combatant meant I had an alternative path that I could take as a conscientious objector, I would have certainly taken it. Proving that I possessed a religious belief and training that might fit the board's definition for classification as a CO, however, might be a different story. As I mentioned before, I was all over the place when it came to religion and I couldn't claim membership or lifelong involvement in one of the peace churches like the Quakers, Amish, Mennonites or Jehovah Witnesses, the more traditional route to becoming a CO based on religious belief.

In fact, my experience with religion stemmed from enjoying the theater in all of it, especially the Episcopal Church with its incense, rituals, and music, and especially the vestments and liturgical garments. Even as a child, I'd attend churches wherever I lived, usually after meeting a new friend when we moved to a new town; I'd either be asked or I inquired to go with them to their place of worship. My parents and younger brother, Mitchell, never went, my dad claiming to be a home Baptist, something he made up. My mother? Maybe an agnostic. There was a string of protestant churches and sects that kept me occupied throughout my childhood and into my teens—Methodist, a couple unaligned community churches, Lutheran, Christian Science, Presbyterian, Episcopal, Unitarian-Universalist. I even played and conducted choirs for services in some, including Holy Cross Roman Catholic Church in Rumson, New Jersey, which I abruptly quit a week before Easter when the priest decided to change the already rehearsed music selected for the services. How dare he! And, during my senior year of high school, when I seemed to be struggling with defining who I was, coming to terms with being gay but unable to speak that truth to anyone, my parents sent me to a reformed rabbi for counseling. I was a spiritual nomad without sanctum, even learning a bit of

Hebrew and thinking of seriously converting to Judaism at one point later in my adult life. I didn't attend church to be filled with a holy spirit, I went to church to be entertained. I couldn't rely on my inconsistent religious upbringing to help me qualify for becoming a conscientious objector. So much for option one.

I also knew that my objection to participating in the war had to encompass participation in all wars, not just the Vietnam conflict, as that would appear to be a political stand, not a religious or moral one. This war was the only war I had to object to at the moment, except for the interior war I was fighting to prove I wasn't going to fight. It was frustrating as hell to continually claim to be a pacifist and have no one with the authority to grant me conscientious objector status to do so, my pleas seemed to always fall on deaf ears. I constantly felt like I was being ignored and not taken seriously.

The Vietnam era prompted greater clarification on the established criteria for claiming conscientious objector status with respect to the draft. The 1948 draft law's definition of conscientious objection to war stipulated that one needed to prove his objection to military service based on religious training and a belief in God in the Judeo-Christian tradition. A 1965 Supreme Court ruling *United States v. Seeger* determined that a CO did not have to demonstrate a firm belief in God, but still needed to show a "sincere and meaningful belief" in something greater than himself that filled the void where God should have been. While that ruling came down in 1965, the court did not include a timeline for its implementation. *Welsh v. United States* was still to be decided by the Supreme Court, but once that ruling was made in 1970, individuals could also seek CO status purely on the "depth and fervor" of their ethical and moral beliefs, so long as they weren't "political or philosophical." That decision would not be handed down until June 15 and local draft boards could, again, interpret the ruling in any way they chose. I hadn't heard about any of these rulings during draft counseling with the Princeton student I spoke to after the university protest in May or with the Central Committee for Conscientious Objectors shortly after that in Philadelphia.

It was too late for me, it seemed, as I had already been denied my request for CO status by my local board in my first appeal as well as my second one at the state level.

Looking back, the Supreme Court ruling *Welsh v. United States* may have played in my favor in my third and final appeal to the national board. If it did, I was never told. Reasons for granting or denying an appeal request were never shared with the one making the appeal. Your appeal was either approved or rejected. Early in the process it felt like I was in a one-way tunnel traveling toward induction with no foreseeable chance to make a U-turn or back out. I needed an ally, someone to speak for me other than an unfeeling file folder. I wanted transparency from those who plotted to control my life. I was looking for mercy but only found callousness.

Option two would have me leaving the country and going into exile. I could move to Canada. I had already filled out the necessary immigration forms and paperwork. I kept this as the very last option, however, as I truly loved the United States and still wanted to do my part, just not in fatigues while carrying a gun. If all else failed and I was left with no other choice, this was what I was willing to do to be true to myself. In Canada at least, I could look across the border and see the land that I loved.

Of the options before me, my parents questioned them all. They worried about and for me. They questioned whether I was ruining my life by refusing to fight in a war. They might, however, deal with me living in Canada. After all, my dad's dad came from Prince Edward Island before moving to Worcester, Massachusetts as a child, but I doubted it.

Option three would be based in truth but came with baggage that I might have to carry around with me for years if I was to admit it. I had a personality disorder according to the Selective Service—"overt homosexuality or other forms of sexual deviant practices such as exhibitionism, transvestism, voyeurism." I could check the box that I was a homosexual, it was still listed as a mental illness, and because of that, an immediate and permanent exclusion from military service. I didn't see this as an acceptable choice even though it could be an easy way out. If so, I would have indicated it during my draft physical months before. Maybe deep down I harbored a greater fear with this option, a fear that lurked if I was exposed as being gay, of having that fact permanently registered as part of my draft physical and placed in a file somewhere. After being 'out' in college—if that's what you called it in the days immediately leading up to and after the Stonewall Riots—and for the most part comfortable with who I was, deep down I dreaded being out beyond the safety of my circle of friends at my small and insulated college. My parents might fear that public disclosure much more than my being a conscientious objector.

Finally, for my fourth option, I could just not show up for induction as ordered or show up but refuse to carry a gun once basic training had begun. Either way, I'd be risking up to five years in federal prison or detained for the same amount of time in some loosely secured civilian work camp.

I already had decided that I would not carry a gun, no matter what. I even refused my father's offered lessons on how to shoot a weapon, his weapon, a handgun he carried as insurance during late night rendezvous at Bethlehem Steel when he was called in to negotiate free passage for one of his company truck drivers during teamster job actions.

I disappointed my father with my refusal to learn from him. He had been a recognized marksman, a sharpshooter in the Massachusetts Militia. He had the medals to prove it. He had wanted to enlist in the regular army during World War II, but was turned away, 4-F, for being deaf in one ear with partial hearing loss in the other, a result of having had scarlet fever as a kid. He was proud of his time serving in the state guard, but down deep he knew his hearing impairment kept him from doing more for the war effort.

I wasn't a draft dodger or a deserter and tried hard not to be seen as such. Maybe I was, in all reality, a coward. Was I taking this action out of fear or anchored in moral obligation? The thing was, I wanted to serve my country. The civically responsible optimist in me thought everyone should be giving two years of service for the collective good, but in ways that would also take advantage of their unique gifts, talents, skills, and abilities. I saw it as a modified Work Progress Administration Federal Art Project so to speak. I didn't see this as merely a government program providing jobs during a period of economic turmoil as with the WPA in the 1930s, but an opportunity for people to give back to the nation, to make a difference using their own talents and gifts, to have purpose and to be of value. I saw examples of what could be a possible national alternative service projects in the WPA murals in the main post office in Allentown and more recently, just a couple of years ago, I came across James Michael Newell's multi-paneled fresco, covering 1,400 square feet, *The Evolution of Western Civilization*, while giving a workshop in the library at Evander Childs High School in the Bronx. The mural was completed in 1938 and Newell enlisted the help of high school students in its creation. I was shocked when I entered the room, amazed it had survived eighty years despite remodeling, recent upgrades to accommodate new technology and more than a few attempts to have it destroyed over the years for political or social reasons. I was awestruck when I saw it, as if glimpsing the Sistine Chapel ceiling for the very first time. This was powerful stuff, I wanted to do powerful stuff, too. If this was what national service could achieve as part of the WPA Federal Art Project, why couldn't it work for the Selective Service work program, too?

My struggle was a moral one. I was faced with an ethical dilemma pitting me as the individual versus the community; a paradigm in staying true to who I was and what I believed versus how I'd go about meeting my civic obligation and heeding my country's call without having to take up arms against another people. As I continued to weigh my options, I desperately wanted to keep those I loved close to me, to help them understand what I was doing, to maintain their trust and belief in me and have them trust that I would do the right thing, but it was hard.

My parents struggled with my decision in seeking a conscientious objector classification from my local draft board. My father did because he was not able to enlist during World War II due to his hearing impairment. Early in the Vietnam conflict and up until shortly after I was drafted, I believe my father, if he could, would've have served with pride in any branch of the armed forces that would take him. He might have harbored the thought of me serving as his proxy in this war. My mother, on the other hand, felt my decision to become a conscientious objector would reap the same public ridicule as being openly gay, and was worried that I'd be shamed, shunned, and stigmatized for the rest of my life.

I shared my father's name, even though my parents never called me by it. I was born Donald Lyle Proffit, Jr., but called Buzzy as soon as I came into the world. The name, the same nickname as my grandfather Lyle's, my dad's dad, who died well before I was born, was given to me as my parents didn't want me to be called *Donnie* or *Junior*, or *Donald* or *Don*, for that matter; the latter two were reserved for my father alone. The first two, *Donnie* and *Junior*, they detested for some reason and didn't want those for me at all. So, I was Buzzy or Buzz and regardless of what I was named, it was expected that I live my life as my dad had—a man of high moral character, respected in the community, and a good provider for his family.

They asked me to join them at the kitchen table on June 2, 1970. I had no idea what for, but noticed them sitting side by side, facing my mother's portable Royal typewriter. She was placing a sheet of carbon paper between two sheets of white paper and then fed them through the feed rollers onto the platen.

"We know that you are being drafted and we know that you are looking for a way to avoid combat in Vietnam," my father was speaking. He held a piece of paper with handwritten notes on it.

Once my mother had the paper in place on her typewriter, she said, "We both wish that you weren't facing this situation, that you were not being drafted, that you could teach music after college as you, I guess, all of us had wanted."

My father continued. "I had always wanted to serve in the Army. It was World War II and it mattered to me, to defend the country, but with my hearing and all, they didn't want me. This war is different, and although what you are doing wouldn't be what I would do, we know that you need follow this through, because you're you."

"So, we're going to write a letter to your draft board saying that we support you and it's difficult for us, and I'm worried for you, but this is what you want," my mother said.

My dad had already sketched out the letter, it was on the piece of paper he held in his hand. He read it aloud as my mother typed. There was always something about the sound of the clicking keys when my mother typed that made me remember how much I loved listening to *The Typewriter* by Leroy Anderson as a kid on an RCA Victor 45 rpm Bakelite phonograph. The short instrumental piece used an actual typewriter played by a percussionist frantically typing away, the end of each musical phrase accentuated by a metallic ping and the sound of the carriage return lever being hit. I sat at the end of the table, my parents sitting together on my right. My mother's tapping on the keys and my father's voice becoming one, a song that would mark this moment forever.

R. D. # 1
Emmaus, Pa. 18049
THE CHAIRMAN
LOCAL DRAFT BOARD #89
118 North Ninth Street
Allentown, Pa. 18102

Mr. Chairman:
This letter is written by the parents of Donald Lyle Proffit, Jr.,

regarding our son's reluctance in becoming involved in activities which could result in the harming of persons not engaged in actual warfare against our country.

The way of life which our son choses to follow is based on his pacifist upbringing, his religious concern, and his personal evaluation of the present world situation.

His home life has been based on the integrity of individual men, the right to contribute their part and obligation to society and mankind in a manner best suited to that individual's character, abilities, religious beliefs and in his psychological ability to be such, as committed to society.

It is our sincere belief that exposure to actual combat where the destruction of lives, not directly in armed combat with our country, could result in irreparable damage to a person who has dedicated his life to the education of children and youth of our country.

We believe our son is truly entitled to seek conscientious objection.

> Very Truly Yours,
> Donald L. Proffit, Sr.
> Naimi M. Proffit (Mrs. D. L. Proffit)

Once to Every Man and Nation

Then it is the brave man chooses while the coward stands aside
—James Russell Lowell *Once to Every Man and Nation*

ON APRIL 30, 1970, PRINCETON STUDENTS and a good number of faculty gathered at the University Chapel to protest Nixon's decision to send troops into Cambodia. The gathering ended with a vote to strike, the first university to do so following Nixon's decision, and launching a student boycott of all classes to begin the next morning. In a matter of days, similar gatherings would spread to universities and colleges across the country, as students and faculties called for a strike and sought a moratorium on classes.

On the night of May 3, the Westminster Symphonic Choir, my college's largest choral group, composed of all sophomores, juniors, and seniors, was performing Beethoven's Ninth Symphony with the American Symphony Orchestra. Our conductor for this performance was the legendary Leopold Stokowski, who I first saw in the mid-1950s in Disney's animated feature film *Fantasia*, as he led the Philadelphia Orchestra through a series of classical music pieces. The exhilarating and highly emotional opus, Beethoven's final work, culminates with the stirring chorale, Ode to Joy, at the end of the fourth movement. Seated on risers and clad in our iconic scarlet robes, we filled the space behind the orchestra on the Carnegie Hall stage. We sat motionless through the first three movements, the four soloists seated on the stage apron before the proscenium and beside the conductor's platform. When the expected fourth movement segue of chordal dissonance balanced with the recitatives in the lower strings and resounding of themes from each previous movement signaled the approaching choral finale, the Ode to Joy, when we were supposed to stand along with the soloists for our part, the maestro put down his baton and turned to face the audience. At first, we didn't know if he was ill, he had turned 88 years old just two weeks earlier, or if something else was wrong that caused him to abruptly stop. It was unheard of to interrupt the sequence of movements in a symphony.

We could only watch in awe as the maestro looked to each section of the audience, from the parquet to the first and second tiers, to the dress circle and balcony, as if trying to see each face and acknowledge every single one of us. Then he spoke. He condemned the recent invasion of Cambodia and then went on to say how the war was a complete antithesis to peace, to the theme of universal brotherhood in the Ode to Joy, to all the young people protesting for an end to the war, *Alle Menschen werden Brüder*. The audience was silent, no dissenting jeer was heard, even though among the more than two thousand in attendance, I'm sure a few would disagree with the maestro's use of his podium as an opportunity to take a politicizing stand in the middle of a Beethoven symphony, but for the moment we were all one.

When he had concluded his remarks, he turned away from the audience, picked up his baton, looked to his orchestra and then to us, a peaceful countenance upon him. We stood, the soloists stood, the orchestra shifted forward in their chairs, his downbeat signaling the last movement of the symphony. As a choir we were one voice, in collective motion, a simultaneous moving entity, a field of red reeds swaying in unison, caught in a current of aural rapture—to this day, the most powerful musical experience of my life. No one would have expected that this emotional high would be all too soon short lived by the very next morning.

On May 4, 1970, exhausted from the performance in New York the night before, I fell in formation with other students as we joined ranks heading across town toward Princeton University's Jadwin Gymnasium, an imposing Buckminster Fuller-inspired sports complex topped by expansive geodesic shells sitting like some otherworldly cathedral to an ivy-draped athlete-god. There were so many of us moving toward the gym (5,000 in all, I'd read the next day in the Daily Princetonian). We sought seats in the asymmetrical splendor of bleachers and tiered balconies, brought together by Nixon's announced invasion of Cambodia just days earlier. The room buzzed in uneasy anticipation. I wanted and needed direction and thought I might find it here, to do something, to act, even though not sure of what that action would or could be. I anticipated discovering my next steps in the words of the student speakers set to address us, or, in some way, I was seeking permission to take a stand along with the others in the room. Seeing the size of the turn out, more people than I'd imagined coming together in one place to voice their opposition to the war, gave me hope and a sense of belonging to a community, of not being alone in my thinking. The experience also began to coalesce my random thoughts and feelings about this war and about all wars. I was sure now, with my low draft lottery number of fifty-eight and the fact I was opposed to this war and would not carry a gun, if I were indeed to be drafted once I graduated from Westminster, I would need a plan in place to successfully maneuver through the next few months. I would also need the support of my parents, or at least help them understand what I was about to do, what my options were. As of early May, I hadn't even talked with them about how I was feeling with respect to the war and the dilemma I faced in serving in the military.

While I sought clarity in all this, it also raised a question of when wars were justified. I'd listened to stories as a young child told to me by my grandfather, my mother's father, about General John Stark of New Hampshire. As a colonel, Stark crossed the Delaware River on Christmas night, 1776, and then fought alongside Washington at the Battles of Trenton and Princeton. The Princeton Battlefield Memorial, just two miles from this protest, was a park I frequented often in spring and fall, enjoying picnic lunches and frisbee tosses. Stark was my fifth great grandfather, his words, *Live Free or Die*, emblazoned on New Hampshire's license plates, came to mind while I moved through the gym. Would he oppose the Vietnam War? Was I opposing my ancestor's part in the Revolutionary War by taking a stand against all wars?

I spotted a few open seats closer to the floor, hoping to save myself the steep climb to the bleachers in the higher rows, when someone handed me a strip of thin manila paper snipped from a news ticker. "Read it and pass it on, spread the news." Other student organizers distributed the same headline snippets to each new wave of students entering the building. As more and more people read and passed along the news, an unsettling silence washed over us, as if someone was intentionally turning down the volume in the gym. The news was bad and came crashing over us like an incoming wave, hitting the lower bleachers first and rising to the rafters above. I lowered my head and read the slip of paper, "4 Kent State Students Killed by Troops."

I walked the several blocks back to Westminster Choir College, a small school with four hundred students who trained in choral music, organ, piano, voice, and music education. The school's compact quad included Williamson Hall on its south side. The building was capped with a white clock tower giving it dominance over the two dorms facing each other across the lawn, East and West Halls. A small chapel situated on the north side completed the square. There was a structural harmony evident in the four buildings. They belonged together all sharing the same restrained Georgian

Revival style. At any hour of the day and night, arpeggios, scales, toccatas, and fugues would leak from basement practice room windows filling the Dutch elm-lined quad in a hazy tonal dissonance never quite finding resolution. We were so small, no Princeton or Rutgers. It reminded me of Brigadoon, protected in a magical mist, lost to some other place and time.

Within a day of the Princeton protest, I joined a few of my classmates to organize our small campus, seeking a modified moratorium on class attendance the last three weeks before graduation. We fashioned armbands by tearing out a strip from the bottom inner hem of our scarlet choir robes, which every student at the college was required to purchase as freshmen and to wear as standard protocol when we performed. We called a meeting in a lecture hall in the library's basement. I think we wanted to see if we had any support among students and faculty and were reassured when the room filled to standing room capacity. I found myself standing on the small lecture platform with three or four other students, who turned and gestured for me to offer remarks to those assembled. Don't remember if we had thought this part out fully, I know I hadn't; we were better at planning than the follow-through. I was petrified, shy beyond words—suddenly infected with a terminal case of stage fright. I had no notes. I had to speak; they were waiting. Those who showed up looked to us for leadership and direction the same way I sought it from the Princeton students who led us to action just the day before at Jadwin Gymnasium. I stepped forward, my remarks stilted and suggested we take a vote. We took a vote for a moratorium on class attendance until graduation for those who wanted that option to continue protesting.

We did not ask for anything more than that as many of us still had to give our senior recitals in the few remaining weeks ahead. We also couldn't interfere with a contracted series of scheduled performances with the New York Philharmonic later in May. We asked for any other suggestions for what we might want to do, how we could be of use—a chapel memorial service for the slain students at Kent State or how we could use our voices in protest. We staged no sit-ins, no verbal attacks, or unreasonable demands of our administration, but held the suggested chapel memorial service to honor the four slain students.

During the service, four of us each memorialized one of the fallen students, Allison Krause, Sandra Lee Scheuer, Jeffrey Glenn Miller, and William K. Schroeder. I was overcome standing at the pulpit when I shared William Schroeder's obituary with the student body, his short life condensed to a few paragraphs that took less than a minute to read. A short-lived life, he was only nineteen, attending Kent State University on an ROTC scholarship, ironically taken down by an Ohio National Guardsman.

I recently came across a few articles marking the fifty-year anniversary of the Kent State shootings. In one article, William's sister recalled how her brother was majoring in psychology that spring semester with the hope of one day serving soldiers returning from combat. How in high school his game was basketball. At age thirteen he was already an Eagle Scout, a significant achievement at that age, and played cornet in Lorain's All City Band. In another article, his roommate mentioned how Bill told him he was scared as military helicopters buzzed over the campus, search lights breaking through darkened dorm windows as students tried to sleep. Two days later he'd be dead, a bullet in his back, fired from the length of a football field away. Our memorial service closed as we sang Peter Lutkin's Benediction, settling in the peace of its seven-fold amen.

One of our agreed-upon actions was to rent a bus so that we could travel to the nation's capital and protest. Early on the Thursday morning of that week we left Princeton for the four-hour drive to Washington. We sang hymns in protest of the war in front of the White House but were abruptly shooed away because we lacked the necessary permit. When this happened, rather than giving up, we immediately regrouped and instead went to the steps of the Capitol and continued our musical disobedience. The Capitol

Police also interceded, looking for a permit. Within their ranks, however, someone must have realized we were from New Jersey and contacted Senator Clifford Case's office.

A few years earlier, in July 1965, President Johnson was moving the country toward a deepening involvement in Vietnam, calling up additional reservists and extending the tours of duty for current military personnel already on the ground. In a speech on the Senate floor in June, Case stated, "so long as our military operations remain compatible with our stated objective of negotiations, there has been no real alternative to our present course, and I have supported that course." By May 1967 after traveling to South Vietnam as a member of the Senate Foreign Relations Committee, his support for the war had shifted. The trip provided him with a new lens in which to view the conflict. With opportunities to meet with South Vietnam government officials and members of the military, he also journeyed to more rural villages to assess what was happening to the people firsthand.

When he returned from this trip, Case's position on the war had changed. He could no longer envision a negotiated peace. He felt the American people were being deceived by the "misleadingly cheerful reports of progress." Case was becoming an outspoken critic of U. S policy and the war, calling for our withdrawal during Nixon's first term in office.

One of the Capitol Police officers came over to pass along a message. We were asked to meet with Senator Case. We were elated; someone had noticed us and passed the word along to our senator. We crossed the street to the Senate Office Building and once inside were escorted to his office where he listened to our concerns. He shared his thoughts on the war and his shift in thinking that had taken place. His words and our presence in his office gave me a sense of hope, a feeling of accomplishment. He asked us to sing for him and his staff.

"Once to every man and nation, comes the moment to decide,
In the strife of truth with falsehood, for the good or evil side;

Some great cause, some great decision, offering each the bloom or blight,

And the choice goes by forever, 'twixt that darkness and that light."

He seemed moved by our sincerity and singing and shortly after, with hymnals in hand, we boarded our bus for the return trip home, feeling satisfied in contributing our voices to the cause, if only in this small way.

Personally, I felt part of something bigger than just the events of the previous week. I felt connected to my classmates and the college in a deeper way. I felt recognized, to have a purpose and be valued for who I was and what I stood for in opposing this war.

* * *

LOCAL BOARD NO. 89
118 N. NINTH STREET
ALLENTOWN, PA. 18102
25 JUNE 1970

Mr. Donald L. Proffit, Jr.
Route #1
Emmaus, Pennsylvania 18049

Dear Mr. Proffit:
SSS 36-89-48-39

The Local Board considered your request for classifica-
tion as a conscientious objector at their June meeting. They
classified you 1-A and you were mailed an SSS Form 110
to that effect. We presume you received it since it was not
returned to us by the Post Office.

We will advise you when and where to meet with the
Appeal Agent and when you can meet with the Local
Board.

The request for occupational deferment from your employer was not received until 23 June 1970. As you know, the Board can grant no new occupational deferments on requests received after 22 April 1970. However, the Board will consider your employer's request.

Very truly yours,
FOR THE BOARD:
(Miss) Mamie C. Bramwell
Executive Secretary

I had run out of student deferments and the occupational deferment request from the Hackley School headmaster for an exemption was rejected by my five-member local draft board made up of local businessmen and farmers, mostly veterans having served in World War II. The rejection for occupational deferment felt like an *oh, and here's some more bad news for you* following the more critical news that I had not been granted conscientious objector status by the board. I was devastated about not being classified 1-O, but I was also disappointed about the Hackley School position. It was to have been my first teaching job in the fall as the school's music teacher. I desperately wanted the position at this school perched high on a palisade above Tarrytown, everything about it appealed to me, the castle-like fortress of gothic structures, views across the Hudson River, and the school head who was the brother of my headmaster at the small boarding school where I had worked in Princeton during college. However, it was not to be. The position was not compelling enough, deemed not essential in a time of war for my local draft board to consider it worthy of an exemption from military service. I'd need to teach math or science for that to happen. I suggested to the headmaster that he consider my former college roommate and best friend, Herb Chamberlain, for the position. He did and Herb got the job. At least it was still in the family. While I was happy that Herb got the job, privately I mourned the loss of something I dearly wanted and felt perfectly suited.

Herb

Allentown, Pennsylvania
July 20, 1970
Dear Herb,

I went for my personal appearance tonight. I was extremely nervous. I told them it is the greatest blasphemy to God to kill or take the life of another human. They appeared sympathetic. I know, though, that I will not be deferred for teaching—the CO claim is my only chance. That option may have been blown tonight, too.

There was an ad in the NY Times for teachers in Australia—too far. Eh—I'm not too worried—whatever happens, happens. I do know that I will not serve regardless of the board's decision (I told them that, too).

The play is coming on fine. The cast is very good—both as people and actors. I do have a rehearsal Friday night at 7:30-9:30 p.m. I will leave after rehearsal and be in Toms River about 12 midnight. If this is too late for you, I can leave on Sat. a.m. I will have to leave on Sun. morning to be back here around 2 p.m. for rehearsal. Let me know by

Friday. Letters usually only take 1 day in transfer.

Allentown is quiet. The band, Chicago, is supposed to play here in August sometime. Will see you this weekend.

Love,
Buzzy

* * *

Freshman year. The first time I heard Herbie's voice was in the Westminster Choir College Playhouse, a large Quonset hut just off the quad and near the chapel, that was used for everything from rehearsals to eurythmics to physical education as well as socials and the May Day Dance. We were big into May Day and even had a maypole erected in the center of the quad, which we danced around, twisting long streamers which were secured to the top of the pole—very festive.

It was the first meeting of the mandatory physical education class that all freshmen were required to take. Our instructor, an ivy leaguer, was this perfect physical specimen snagged by Westminster from the ranks of Princeton undergraduates. He wanted us to introduce ourselves. He had no clue of where we came from or who we were but was charged with making sure we met some health and fitness requirement. He was up for a challenge dealing with us. Most of us feared breaking a finger in some random game of tag with a soccer ball, which would prevent us from playing organ or piano; for me, I wanted to avoid exposure lest I be tagged as different. Though I looked athletic and was often picked as a team captain, I feared any type of group competitive sports, not because I wasn't capable or enjoyed the game, but because I was gay and didn't want to risk a locker room scene where I'd be accused of staring at a disrobed classmate or worse. It really didn't matter here, though. We didn't have a locker room and there were others just like me trying to protect, conceal, disguise, or hide their difference. Anyway, we each had to introduce ourselves to the class. All I know is that when it was Herbie's turn to introduce himself, who

I couldn't see as he was hidden by the others toward the end of the row, his voice went right through me, a powerful reaction. I had never experienced anything like it, more like a shock wave hitting my ears and echoing someplace deep inside me. It was his voice that stopped me, cutting through the rest of the student introductions as he stated his name, where he was from and favorite sport. I couldn't see him from where I was sitting, but nevertheless, his voice got to me. Where was he from? That accent, so soft, it seemed to drift between a drawl and a twang, and it bothered me in an intriguing sort of way, South Jersey.

Later that same day on the third floor of North Hall, my roommate, Bart, who was also gay, and I were meandering through the hallway, stopping in a few dorm rooms to get better acquainted with our classmates. We stopped in one of the freshmen rooms a couple doors down from ours. There he was along with his roommate, Richard. For some reason Herb had nothing on, standing on a chair, stretching, and placing folded clothes in the upper storage cabinet above the closet. He was so at ease. Bart and I caught each other's eyes. I think I nearly swooned. I know I lost my breath for a moment. I remember how beautiful his skin was. I had never seen anyone so beautiful. Then he spoke, and the same feeling came over me from earlier in the day when I heard that voice in the Playhouse, but now I had a face and body to go with it. I fell in love at that moment.

Alaska Children's Services

Allentown, Pennsylvania
September 22, 1970
Dear Herb,

   AH! What a day! Two letters from Selective Service today. One a form, the other (was I overcome!), my 1-O classification card indicating that I was morally opposed to serving in the military in any way. I didn't think I would get it. But there it was. I read the card for a second time to be absolutely sure I hadn't confused a 1-A for a 1-0 through my tears. *My mother was standing by me at the end of the driveway when I got the mail. I think she thought I was overreacting. I then reread the first letter and attached form. I had just a few weeks to secure an approved job and be ready to report for alternative service duty at 8:00 sharp on November 1.*

   There are some schools and orphanages in Penna., also two in Alaska. Alaska also needs someone in a jr. college. Orphanages up there are mostly Indian children. I'm calling four places in Alaska tomorrow. The minister at St. Margaret's in Emmaus gave me the name of the bishop up

there, William Gordon—wants me to get in touch with him.
He also mentioned a Father Eddy at St. Mary's in Anchorage.
He never met him but spent a July there serving as the priest
while Eddy was on vacation.

I still must consider Alaska very seriously. A great dis-
tance. Two towns would be Sitka and Haines. Also, an open-
ing here, in the state capital, Harrisburg, Pa.

Although if I got a job in Pennsylvania, I could get to see
you occasionally, more than up North.

I enjoyed our visit Sunday. I feel 100% better. Somehow,
we will get together before I leave. I cannot stay in Allentown
they tell me. I need to find a job at least fifty-five miles from
home as serving the country needs to be a "hardship."

Thank you for the letter to Selective Service—without it I
could not have won. I will write again this week. Be prepared
for a sudden visit.

Love,
Buzzy

I continued working with the Central Committee for
Conscientious Objectors (CCCO), who had helped Muhammad
Ali and Arlo Guthrie apply for CO status. Both men were denied
CO classification by their respective local draft boards. While
Guthrie was never drafted due to a high draft lottery number,
284, Ali was, but refused to serve, claiming to be a conscientious
objector regardless of his local board's decision. Ali questioned
why he should be sent to kill the people of Vietnam while Black
Americans were being denied their human rights at home. It
took the United States Supreme Court to overturn that decision
in a unanimous ruling in Ali's favor, granting him conscientious
objector status.

I needed to find an approved alternative service job and I
needed to do that immediately. The CCCO referred me to an
organization, American Friends Service Committee (AFSC),

that they partnered with in counseling men pursuing conscientious objector classification. Both organizations were based in Philadelphia, a 90-minute drive from Allentown, so it was easy for me to spend a day in Philly and work with both the CCCO and AFSC. The latter organization, however, was instrumental in helping me find an approved alternative service employer that my local draft board would accept. I'd spend hours during each visit searching through the AFSC's approved job bank. Each time paging through the listings, I would find myself pausing on positions in Alaska. I had told Herb that I was seriously considering finding a job there yet wondered what it was that kept drawing my attention to that state. I could only think that it stemmed from the Episcopal priest in Emmaus, Packard Okie, who had suggested I connect with the Bishop of Alaska or a Father Eddy in Anchorage for a possible job. Or maybe I was just looking for a new start in a new place far from home. I didn't call the bishop or connect with the priest, instead, I continued to rifle through the AFSC's list of alternative service positions looking for the right fit.

I wanted to work with children, a teaching job would be a good choice, something that I knew I could do and was passionate about. I loved the learning process and being part of it, watching children engage in the act of worldmaking right in front of me. But there were few teaching jobs listed, and none involved music. There was work in hospitals and a Quaker mission where "volunteers will secure suitable jobs . . . while living in a close-knit group within the ghetto. Funds earned will be pooled and subsistence wages returned from the pool to the participants." You also had to "express in tangible ways one's personal commitment to Christ." Then I noticed a few jobs that involved working with children in Alaska and that appealed to me. It was a place I knew very little about aside from it becoming our 49th state just a decade earlier, and that intrigued me. Alaska would be something new, something different, at the frontier, and that called to me.

ALASKA CHILDREN'S SERVICES, INC.
4600 ABBOTT ROAD
Anchorage, Alaska 99502
September 23, 1970

Mr. Don Proffit
RR #1
Emmaus, Pennsylvania 18049

Dear Mr. Proffit:

I am writing in response to our telephone conversation this morning. The position for which you are applying is that of Relief Cottage Group Counselor between two of our agencies, the one being the Lutheran Youth Center in Wasilla (which is s residential treatment center for ten boys) and the other being the Anchorage Children's Christian Home in Anchorage (which provides emergency shelter care for up to ten children). The Relief Cottage Group Counselor spends three days working at LYC and two at ACCH. The position requires that you to live in. Room and board would be provided you at both agencies, with your semipermanent residence at the Lutheran Youth Center in Wasilla.

The position of Cottage Group Counselor is a demanding one and requires a person who is sensitive to the needs of children in his care. He must be able to engage children in meaningful relationships and activities. The Counselor must be willing to look at himself closely and accept the supervision of a trained social worker and work with others in a team relationship.

If you are interested in the position, please fill out the enclosed application and return it to me. Your transportation will be paid to the job, and your salary will be $400 per month plus your room and board.

*Thank you for your cooperation. I hope to hear from you
in the very near future.*

> *Sincerely,*
> *Kenneth Fallon*
> *Director of Program Services*

I filled out the application and sent it back to Ken Fallon the
next day. The application included a prompt for a personal statement on why I wanted this job, other than the fact that I needed
it to fulfill my alternative service two-year work requirement. The
prompt described the kinds of kids I'd be working with if I got
the job.

"We are working at the Jesse Lee Home with children who are
sometimes highly disturbed. They are not always cute, lovable,
loving little things. Sometimes they are stubbornly hostile, with-
drawn and distant, semi-delinquent, impudent, loud, unmannerly,
provocative, manipulating, quarrelsome and cruel. Knowing all of
this, are you still interest in this position? Why?"

I thought with my background working at the boys boarding
school in Princeton and the fact that I had volunteered one night
to sing with a group of incarcerated boys at the Skillman School, a
newly built state-run youth detention center and training school,
might have prepared me for the job. I submitted my statement
highlighting my passion for working with children that perhaps
was more suited to applying for a music teaching position in a
public school. I got the job but might not have been as prepared
for what the responsibilities for working with kids in crisis really
entailed, even after singing and playing the banjo for a group of
tough kids living out sentences in a New Jersey youth correctional
"cottage." One night of volunteer work at the Skillman School, I'd
soon discover, did not equal having even a basic understanding of
what these kids were going through, what their needs were or how
to support them.

The Road North

MY MOTHER STOOD BY THE KITCHEN DOOR, silent and sad, her glacial blue eyes, a few shades lighter than mine, made no contact as I looked back at her through the rear-view mirror. Binoculars hanging from her neck, her daily accessory for spotting birds or keeping tabs on the coming and going of the paperboy with the German surname, our neighbor, convinced he was a 12-year-old Nazi. She waited until I started the car and then retreated.

Because we moved every two years for almost eight years after my ninth birthday, I would be reluctant to make new friends in each new town we'd find ourselves in, still grieving the friends I left behind and fearing the loss of new ones should we move again, which we seemed to always do. This reluctance to socialize at first was balanced with the ease in which I could break off relationships. The frequency of the moves—we were part of the American middle class family migrations taking place in the 1950s and 1960s, always looking for better paying jobs and better places to live—enabled me to build an emotional barrier from being hurt when I left those friends that I loved. This was not the case now that I looked back, both through the rearview mirror and in my memory, at the woman standing alone in the driveway, her own barrier in place. I had made the decision to experience something new, something distant, a chance to start fresh. With the promise and excitement of a new adventure on America's last frontier as I fulfilled my civilian service obligation, I found that my heart was also breaking for the people and way of life I was about to leave behind.

My mother always knew, as mothers often do, that her first born was queer. Sometimes she was accusatory of why I chose this boy or that as a friend or questioned what we were doing in the woods for so long, always suspecting I fooled around with anyone I brought home. She piled on the guilt as needed, tempered by raising a child in the McCarthy era, homosexuality a national threat. If I was indeed a queer, which I was, she feared, in her way of caring, that my life would be a solitary one filled with sadness. I'd never be the teacher I'd trained so hard to be during college, never be able to run for public office, not that I ever thought I'd want to. With all my dreams dead ended I'd be mocked by others, branded for life, always the outcast. Now I was embarking on this journey as a conscientious objector, something she equally worried would have the same outcome.

The October sun sifted through what remained of fading fall foliage. Maple and oak leaves in reds and yellows framed the gravel driveway leading up to the dirt road that connected to the route off the mountain, past the Nazi's house and down to Emmaus. The car, a '69 green VW Beetle, was packed inside and out with what I thought necessary for my journey and two years stay as far away as I could get from here. Little did I know I had set a course that would alter my life in ways I could not then imagine.

On the inside of the car were books, as many as I could fit and still have room for heavy boots, my Pete Seeger-styled longneck Bacon banjo, maps, a camera, thermal long underwear, layers of coats and sweaters, and my order to report for alternative service. On the outside a tower of spare tires teetered, strapped to the roof rack, for the transcontinental trip north to Alaska. Aside from New

England, New York, and New Jersey and where we lived now in
Allentown and the two years we lived in a small town southwest of
Chicago, I had seen very little else of the country. There was a trip
to Florida when I was three, but all I can remember of that is a few
palm trees and a sandy sink hole behind the cottage rental in Ft.
Myers. What lay beyond the Mississippi River was a mystery to me.

Before getting on Route 22 just north of Allentown, I stopped
by my father's office to say goodbye. My father ran a trucking company which specialized in hauling large structural pieces of iron
and steel, bridge girders and the massive beams that supported the
new twin towers of the World Trade Center in Lower Manhattan. I
knew this place well having worked summers creosoting the wood
decks of flatbed trailers, escorting wide loads, and running errands
to fetch replacement truck parts.

He got up from his desk, straightened his glasses and adjusted
the volume of his hearing aid. A quick handshake and a wish for
good luck sent me away, both of us wanting to say something
more, but unable to find the words. Perhaps it was how my mother
demanded to be the sole conduit of all information to my dad for
both my brother and me that stifled any deep communication
between us. This need to protect my dad seemed to be a thing that
surfaced during our teenage years, when childhood innocence
began to erode. Whenever we faced a situation that would benefit from his wisdom directly, she would intercede and do the bid-
ding for us. "Don't bother your father with that, he works hard and
deserves some peace and quiet when he gets home," was a common response that taught me early on to rely on her for the things
that troubled me, except for the one thing that troubled me the
most: who I really was.

It wouldn't be until after my mother died that my father and
I could build the kind of relationship that allowed us to deeply
confide in each other. We'd talk about his desire to serve during
World War II, to be a soldier, and how his hearing prevented it, and
my being a conscientious objector, because it was the only thing I

could be in wartime. As the Vietnam war came to an end, he had become proud of my stance in opposing it yet serving in the way that I did. "You paid your dues," he would often say.

Where I was most surprised was his stance on my being gay. He accepted it and supported me in any way he could. We'd even spent a long weekend in New York City, his treat, staying in a suite at the Waldorf-Astoria. He wanted to go to the places I went, see where I accompanied dance classes at the Martha Graham Center of Contemporary Dance on East 63rd Street, have a Fanny burger at Great Aunt Fanny's on Restaurant Row and see a couple of shows. It was and still is one of the best times of my life.

I left my dad's office to begin a ten-day trip through Pennsylvania, Ohio, Indiana, Illinois, Wisconsin, Minnesota, and North Dakota. Then I'd turn right once I got to Minot, and steer toward Canada.

* * *

I WROTE LETTERS TO HERBIE ON HOLIDAY INN STATIONERY— Chicago on Lake Shore Drive and in Moorhead, Regina, and Edmonton. As I travelled further north, the letterhead shifted to Travelodges in Dawson Creek and Whitehorse. Each letter relayed highlights from the day's drive, touching on faces that struck me as beautiful, road hazards, loneliness and how much I missed him, us.

There was no us. Although we had explored a more physical relationship when we first met, there came a point when that part of our relationship changed. It was particularly evident between our junior and senior years during an early summer road trip along the New England coast. We spent nights together on a boat in Barnstable Harbor, camped out in Provincetown and Arcadia where the lack of intimacy, and my increasing frustration of not being able to act on my feelings toward Herb, signaled his rejection. We were now just friends. I knew this, yet the more I drove westward, the more solitude I began to experience in the cramped

VW, and the more time I had to convince myself that there was still some promise of us sharing our lives together once my two-year service was over.

Holiday Inn
Lake Shore Drive
Chicago, Illinois
October 23, 1970

Dear Herb,

It's about 1 p.m. (2 p.m. your time). I got into Chicago early. I'll probably go out to eat with Barbara-Barbara. I have a room on the 22nd floor overlooking Lake Michigan— revolving dining room on the top floor.

I'm curious as to what you are up to. I'm about up to the 22nd floor.

Chicago is a nice place. Brings back memories of being 15-17 years old when I went to high school in Tinley Park. I think the sun is shining. Smog and haze.

I miss you very much. My only worry is not seeing you. Don't forget me.

Love
Buzzy

Holiday Inn of Moorhead
Moorhead, Minnesota
October 24, 1970

Dear Herb,

Tonight, I'm just outside Fargo, North Dakota (if you are keeping track). Tomorrow I should be in Regina, Saskatchewan. I'm becoming very lonely now that I have been out three days—almost like going to the moon by your-self. I sometimes feel so very small. Please (I really know *better than to say this, but—) don't ever forget me while I'm gone. And please try not to give me up for another. Sounds foolish, as it were, but it somehow helps me to write it down and get the thoughts out of my head and let you know that I miss you so very much.*

Last night I was able to get a third row seat on the aisle for HAIR! $9.90. Barbara went with (on her own). It was a rather good show. I only wish we could see it together some-time. One guy kept doing Bette Davis imitations. It was all camp, gay, and wild. Good singing. Dancing was superb. New York show, it is said, during the nude scene at the end of Act I makes it so that you really can't see anything, but not in Chicago. Nothing special or pretty. The opening of the show is done in slow motion. It was amazing how they moved so well, so smoothly, so slowly. Strange.

I have seen a lot of flat land today. Minnesota is a flat and strange place. North Dakota should be interesting also.

I think I'll watch TV before I go to bed. I miss you. I think I will start my new journal tonight. I'll write again tomorrow.

Love
Buzzy

The drive from Moorhead to Minot was flat and uneventful and when I got to Minot, I turned right and headed toward Canada. Once at the border, I had hoped for more. With the number of men reluctant to serve in this war, many were in hiding, while others fled across the border to Canada, something that I had strongly considered. So, here I now sat at said border, maybe secretly wanting to be questioned, suspected, at least to have my papers checked, my car searched. There was some part of me, the quiet rebel in me, channeling Stephen Dedalus, the James Joyce protagonist in *Portrait of the Artist as a Young Man*. In my disappointment, I imagined myself standing atop the piled tires on the VW's roof and shouting Stephen's words, "I will tell you what I will do and what I will not do. I will not serve that in which I no longer believe, whether it call itself my home, my fatherland, or my church: and I will try to express myself in some mode of life or art as freely as I can and as wholly as I can, using for my defence, the only arms I allow myself to use — silence, exile and cunning." Instead, I settled for a smile from the border patrol agent, who never left the comfort of his guard house, but remained seated at his desk behind the sliding glass transaction window. Asking only my name and how much money I was carrying, he merely waved me on, quickly sliding shut the glass partition.

Holiday Inn
777 Albert Street
Regina, Saskatchewan, Canada
4:45 p.m.
October 25, 1970

Dear Herb,
Land of the Maple Leaf—pretty flag—colorful money. Regina is the capital of the province. Good sized city. Still flat land everywhere. I should be in Edmonton tomorrow. Customs was a ball—all they asked me was my name and how much money I had with me. I think today I am almost halfway (or at least) halfway there. I must be crazy when I could have stayed in Harrisburg, PA or perhaps N. Y. State. Here I am, so there is a reason for it. Wish we were together. I think I'll shower and go to dinner.
Gas is becoming very expensive—a while ago it cost me 52¢ a gallon—and the gallons here are smaller than they are in the States.
I saw an eagle today standing on the side of the road— plus two dead porcupines and many smelly skunks.
There was a radio station that read the comics over the air this morning. Very camp style—two men—Lil' Abner,

Blonde, the works, then they played some Sophie Tucker and
Rudy Valle records, plus some old Red Skelton Radio Shows.
Until later. I miss you.

Love
Buzzy

I wrote Herbie each night on the journey, mile markers ticking off confessions of my day on the road.

Ditched

T HE NEXT MORNING, I ROSE EARLY AGAIN and dragged my duffle back into the Volkswagen. I forgot to physically check out of the Holiday Inn even though they had taken an imprint of my credit card, well, my dad's card really, the night before. I guess I had done that in Moorhead and Chicago, because when I called home later that day once I got to Edmonton, my father, not using his "gee, son, it's good to hear your voice" tone, let me know he was annoyed having to accept collect calls from hotels to approve the charges for my one-night stays.

Once on the road I found another radio station with excellent programming. This one touched on all my favorite musical styles and genres. I heard a piece by the late Romantic German composer, Richard Strauss, followed by a folk song, followed by an orchestral piece conducted by Benjamin Britten, a real favorite of mine, followed by the Rolling Stones. I was zipping along the highway in a great mood, the music, at least for the moment, taking my mind off feeling lonely and thinking about the next two years of my life serving as a conscientious objector.

Somewhere between Regina and Edmonton on a desolate stretch

of prairie highway the wind screamed. I drove headlong into a fierce flash storm, a snow squall really, that took the horizon and shadows with it, leaving only white. Losing control, I crossed lanes into oncoming traffic, my car blown into a ditch on the other side of the road. Then it was over. Clambering out of the car, I could see that I was not the only one who had been caught by surprise—a half dozen cars guttered and spun in opposite directions lay all around me.

Getting back into the car, I attempted to drive out of the ditch and up onto the highway, but the car was wedged tightly against the steeply sloped sides of the drainage gully, unable to move forward or backward. Leaving the car, locking the door, I stood by the side of the road looking for something hopeful. I noticed what could be a small town, buildings at a crossroads to the west, in the direction I was headed. Crossing back to the other side of the road, I began hitchhiking toward the structures. Recalling my mother's warning before I left home not to pick up hitchhikers or ever hitchhike for fear of being eaten by cannibals. She was referring to a recent report of a young man in Colorado or some other western state, having been devoured by a stranger he picked up on the side of the road. I stuck out my thumb.

An old rust-blemished blue pickup truck with a man and his son slowed as they approached the scene, not to offer me the kindness of a ride, but to take stock of the debris scattered along the highway. I had been ignored in my time of need and I wasn't having it. As the truck passed, I leaped onto the rubber tread of the running board, gripping the door handle for balance and entry. Wrenching it open, I slid onto the seat shoving the boy against his father's side, both startled with the unexpected intrusion.

"Sorry, sorry, sorry. You've got to help me. I just got blown off the road, my car is now on the other side stuck in that ditch." I pointed to the drainage trench running alongside the road. "I'm not from here." I think they realized that fact. I was frantic and panicking. "Please, I've got to get to the nearest gas station and find someone with a tow truck."

Rather than being bounced to the curb, the man cautiously obliged, his sense of responsibility and compassion winning out while the boy stared straight ahead and said nothing.

"I'll help. There's a garage a bit further up the road, but you got to know how you scared the both of us."

I sat back against the sagging bench seat, feeling every spring beneath the ripped and ratty vinyl, my left side pressed hard against the boy in the cramped cab. I exhaled a breath that felt like I had been holding since being thrown off the road. The boy seemed to relax as I began to breathe normally. I looked over at the two of them finally realizing what I had done.

"I'm sorry. That's not like me to do what I just did to you."

He took me to the next intersection, a crossroads with two tall grain elevators and a working garage. He dropped me off at the side of the road and by the time I turned to thank him, he had already taken off, kicking up slush and small stones in his wake.

* * *

ENNIS' NAME WAS STITCHED IN RED ON THE OVAL PATCH of his denim blue-striped herringbone coveralls. The mechanic tried wiping the grease from his hands, fingers, and nails, his palms permanently smudged and immune to the melt away action of Boraxo. He smelled of powdered hand soap and gasoline.

"Hi, I just skidded off the road and my car is trapped in the trench alongside the highway. Some kind of crazy storm. It was like I had no control and now I can't get it out." I told him what had taken place up the road, that not just me, but a few others had been swept up in the freakish squall, a menacing mix of snow, wind and black ice, our vehicles scrambled in the ditch.

"Hold on a second, I'll get my keys." Ennis finished wiping his hands as best he could, looked at them and shrugged and grabbed his coat.

Riding back in his tow truck, I found that it took little effort for

Ennis to pull me out and then to right the remaining cars. Once it was done, I drove back to the garage and paid my share of the cost for being rescued. Then, to dissuade someone like me from forcing their way into my car when least expected, as I had just done to the man and his son in the blue pickup, I pulled my duffel bag from the back, propped it up in the passenger seat, and placed a hat on top to resemble a passenger, signaling to any backpacked-laden drifters along the highway that this car held no promise or room for a free ride.

* * *

I CONTINUED DRIVING LATE INTO THE NIGHT, arriving in what I thought was the most beautiful city I had ever seen, Edmonton. It dazzled in the twilight of a crystal-clear sky, tall buildings glittering like some unexpected Oz at the end of the prairie. Checking into the Holiday Inn, I boarded an elevator, flanked by drunk members of a visiting Soviet hockey team. Or was it the Moscow Ice Circus on tour? We jostled in a turbulent attempt to communicate, but found words useless, except for one, and when it was uttered somewhere in the chaos, I understood. *Wodka* meant vodka. From their mimed gestures of taking shots, I realized they wanted me to join them for a drink. A chime signaled arrival at their floor, doors slid open, men spilled into the hallway as if entering an ice hockey rink with me shuttled like the puck in some pregame warmup drill. I don't remember much during or after that improvised soiree except somehow stumbling back to my room, fumbling with the key, falling into bed, and cuddling up against my mute duffel companion.

Somewhat hung over and still on east coast time, I woke up way too early and headed off for Dawson Creek, the official start of the Alaska Canadian Highway. With a destination ahead and a deadline in getting there to meet, I was beginning to discover that my journey wasn't just about getting from point A to point B, but also a series of adventurous encounters along the way.

Then, somewhere on the other side of Fort St. John the smoothness of asphalt I'd enjoyed since leaving the gravel driveway of my Pennsylvania home abruptly ended. From that point on, the rubbled roadway snapped beneath my tires sending stones and dust skyward. The constant ping of pebbles hitting the car left dimpled dents where before green paint sheened perfection. This would be the roadway surface until I crossed the Yukon-Alaska border where asphalt pavement returned.

Milepost 462

I PULLED INTO THE ROADHOUSE, it might have been called the Highland Glen Lodge, at Milepost 462, roughly halfway between Dawson Creek and Whitehorse. A solitary structure resting alongside the road on Muncho Lake, the Northern Rockies holding it all in place. The roadhouse included rooms, a café, gas, and oil if needed. I found my room, hand-hewn timbers, an aging orange, and cigarette-smoked patina—rustic, distant and familiar. It was off the main dining room. It reminded me of the knotty pine paneling of my childhood home, the one my father built in central Massachusetts not far from the New Hampshire border. Window coverings of hand-sewn curtains, floral, faded and dated, concealed what looked to be a small family gravesite or pet cemetery carved out of the woods behind the building.

Making my way to the dining room, a square room with a few tables offset by a counter for five, I checked the menu.

"Take care in what you pick," the innkeeper warned. "Whatever I take out of the freezer will be the meal for everybody tonight."

I thought for a moment. "What did you have last night?"

"Moose."

What a responsibility, but I wondered if anyone else would really be stopping by. I scanned the menu. A meat, vegetable, and potato. No salad listed, just coleslaw. I picked pork chops, corn, and French fries.

He opened the freezer chest, pulled out a carefully wrapped bundle of chops, reached for an industrial size can of corn, and readied a pile of potatoes for frying, the harvest for family and strangers, or whoever might find themselves dining here tonight.

"First one here picks the meal for everybody this time of year. Not too many pass by now that it's getting colder, darker, except for regular route truckers, and not many of them either."

I wanted to ask him about the graves behind the roadhouse. Were they dead beloved dogs or people or random strangers who fell ill or worse along the way? Or maybe they were just random rocks that had spilled down the hillside that I wanted to be more. I called for a beer instead.

The meal took time as I did my best to navigate an uneasy intimacy between strangers. Waiting for the pork to thaw, I considered the man behind the counter routinely preparing the meal. For him it was home, for me just a diversion, a shelter on an isolated road, a brief stop along the way toward two years of mandatory alternative service without any form of basic training to prepare me.

I ordered another beer as a group of men stormed through the door, their diesel engines idling, waiting outside. Big burly men, walrus-like, braved the Alcan in winter. They huddled like a team, backslapping and butt smacking each other before settling down to eat. It frightened me, this ritual, this closeness, this camaraderie I'd never know. Their collective scent from a long day on the road competed with the aromas rising from the grill and deep fryer. Thinking back on how familiar this all seemed, it reminded me of my Guthsville Playhouse stint in *Man of La Mancha* three months earlier, where a summer stock Cervantes set the scene of a rundown inn, a roadhouse, filled with *rough men—muleteers*, banging their mugs on tables taunting the enticing kitchen wench, Aldonza. I played one of those muleteers, effectively I might add, but this production was a different reality. I would be any one of these truckers' Aldonza for the night, lusting as I was at the sight of them, but lacking the courage to do anything about it trying to survive.

This was not the best time for me to engage in voyeuristic pleasure, the offered scene before me triggered a certain hunger that I needed to quell. Not here, not now. I could have watched them all night, but when one of the younger men casually caught me staring, I carelessly continued to hold his gaze for just a second too long, enough time possibly to get in trouble, then swallowed the rest of my beer and stole away to my room.

I should have known better, especially since I'd had training in how to sit at a bar without staring at men. Mandatory behavior at mafia-controlled, and police-enforced, Greenwich Village taverns, Julius's and Stonewall, just prior to the riots. These places expected its patrons to look straight ahead, no cruising, or you'd find yourself booted to the curb and often carted off in the back of a paddy wagon. You were to keep your life a secret even though everyone knew why you were there and who you really were, you still pretended that you were straight. We seemed to all share the same secret life.

Spurred by a day's solitary confinement in their cabs, the truckers grew boisterous. Leeching from the lodge's dining room, their voices wandered the hall to my room like unwelcome phantoms and suspended themselves in a looping lullaby of gruff voices and rough talk above my head. I sought distraction by reading a few pages from one of the books I packed for the journey. Picking up where I had left off the night before and somewhere halfway through James Baldwin's *Another Country,* my breath caught on the sentence where Baldwin describes the fallacy of believing he is living a secret life and how it's only a secret to himself and not at all to those around him, who know him or who encounter him each day. For those who see the secret before the dissembler does, they have a way of laying him bare, sometimes to cause harm, sometimes not. One sentence on one page seemed to sum up my life at that moment.

* * *

FLESH EATER. THAT'S WHAT I WAS CALLED during my junior year of high school. It was whispered to me and about me during class, louder in the halls where it was safer to shout it and then retreat unseen into the hundreds of kids changing classes. Tinley Park High School was a large school serving a community surrounded by corn and soy fields in southwest Cook County.

We moved to Illinois when I was fifteen, leaving behind the affluence and prestige of Greenwich, Connecticut, where we lived in a converted carriage house and struggled to meet the rent. Chicago held better opportunities for my dad at the time, so off we went.

Tinley Park is where I learned to drive on my mother's '63 VW red convertible. It's also where I joined the school's band, a Sousa-styled force capable of invading small towns on the Fourth of July riding on a complicated street cadence and striking awe in the bleachered crowds during halftime at football games. I played the Scottish tenor drum during marching band season, bigger and more cumbersome than a snare, a struggle to keep it balanced on my knee when marching, the kind usually found in Scottish pipe and drum bands. The sound, however, was riveting, went to your core. During the winter I played tympani in the concert band. The band room is where I found sanctuary, the halls and classrooms a certain hell for me, especially after becoming friends with Tucker, a senior.

Tucker played trumpet during concert band season and was the charismatic drum major when we were marching or performing halftime routines when he'd belt out commands, blast his American Thunderer whistle and signal charges with his mace. Tall, a varsity wrestler, too, and extremely popular with a beautiful cheerleader girlfriend, Tucker was recognized throughout the high school.

I found myself in bed with him one night. A few of us from band and chorus had formed a folk singing group and were performing at a ski lodge overlooking the Mississippi River near Galena, our payment for our time and talent was free lodging and meals for the night.

After our performance and once we were in our respective rooms, mine shared with Hugh, now asleep, and Tucker, wide awake. The two of us engaged in whispered conversation. Tucker and I sharing the one double bed while Hugh snored softly on the rollaway cot next to us.

I maneuvered our conversation toward boys having sex with each other; I think it was mostly about oral sex. Excited and ready to go further, I asked if he had ever done it with a guy. I don't remember his answer, but I do remember that he said I could do it to him. He must have had some previous encounter with this activity, maybe with the cheerleader, as he instructed me on the proper technique he was expecting. More than the act, I remember how Tucker smelled, his sweat, somehow metallic and his immediate silence after we were done.

Leaving the room the next morning, Hugh, who I thought had peacefully slept through the night, commented only once, saying, "I didn't think you were that way." I never asked him what he meant, nor did he ever mention it again.

As for Tucker, several weeks later we were out driving around after school, it was spring. I parked my mother's red VW on the side of the road in a rural southwest corner of Cook County, shielded by the previous seasons decaying stalks of corn. Tucker and I had one more awkward attempt at intimacy, me on my knees straddled between pavement and roadside gravel, Tucker in the back seat of the VW. I didn't fear being noticed should someone happen to drive by, it didn't seem to occur to me, consumed as I was with what was about to happen. However, our pleasure was short-lived as we were interrupted by an eerie green sky and sudden stillness in the air signaling an approaching tornado, the distant town's sirens wailing out its warning to take immediate cover.

The next day in school, during second period English class, I heard someone say, "flesh eater," just a whisper. I heard it again, a little more volume behind it this time. I turned to my left, trying to see who said it and saw two wrestlers, both juniors on the varsity team with Tucker looking straight at me, big smiles turning into sneers. They were directing the words at me. I knew immediately I had been found out. I could only suspect that my new label came from Tucker and the team as I became the topic of some seamy locker room talk. If I had been living a secret life before, that life was now over for me in this town.

* * *

I WOKE THE NEXT MORNING WAY BEFORE dawn, the hour of the wolf, the time between the dark of night and light of day. F. Scott Fitzgerald provides a specific hour for what he calls the dark night of the soul where it is always 3:00 a.m. day after day. I had seen Ingmar Bergman's 1968 psychological horror film, *The Hour of the Wolf*, at Princeton's Garden Theater shortly after its release. In a screenplay note, Bergman explains the hour of the wolf as a period of time, a few hours really, that stretches from midnight to dawn; the hours when most people die, and sleep is deepest, and nightmares release the ghosts and demons that remain hidden during the day.

Not keeping up with each new time zone I crossed, I was now waking up during the hour of the wolf as my internal clock seemed stuck on eastern standard time.

After a shower, the warm water rinsing away any remaining ghosts from the night before, I gathered my things and stuffed them back inside my duffel. It was a little before 4:00 a.m.. I pulled back the homemade cotton curtains and peered through the window. It was raining, cold but not yet icing the outside surfaces.

I made my way toward the dining room, placing the room key on the counter. I heard kitchen noises in the back and before

I could reach the door to leave, the cook appeared with a cup of coffee.

"Here, you'll want this before you head out. You're crossing rugged terrain today. Need to be alert."

"Thanks," I said, dropping my duffel by the door and returning to the counter to wrap my hands around the warm mug.

"Breakfast? It's early for me to be open, but I'm up and you're about ready to head out without eating."

"Thanks," I said again, climbing onto a stool at the counter.

As I ate, he told me about the road ahead along the Toad, Trout and Laird Rivers, where to stop for gas, what to expect crossing the remaining northern section of the Canadian Rockies and how I would be traversing the British Columbia-Yukon border a few times before the final stretch into Whitehorse. A daunting trip, but nevertheless doable in these last few days of October, weather permitting. I was ready for it.

Breakdown I

I T WAS STILL DARK WHEN I DROVE AWAY, the lodge discernible in my rearview mirror. An incandescent light emanated from the dining room's thermal pane windows that framed silhouettes of men eating breakfast. The same light reflected off the cabs of the tractor trailers remaining in the lot. I eased into the solitude of the gravel roadway, knowing that the distance between settlements would now be hours apart. I turned on the radio but only picked up static, remembering that I had lost any reception somewhere outside of Dawson Creek the day before. The rain only slightly tempered the dust and gravel wake of my car. The risk to any driver in trouble during this time of year was considerable. Traffic was significantly lighter as winter approached, with only a few trucks, and even fewer cars, making the journey in either direction. The chance for someone stopping to offer help in case of need, was remote. That was something I could not afford; I had a deadline to make. November 1 was just a few days away, adding any extra time to this trip due to an unexpected mishap would delay my arrival and I was worried that my draft board would discover it. Could a conscientious objector be considered AWOL by failing to show up for duty on time?

With nearly five hundred miles between here and Whitehorse, I knew I was in for a good ten-hour day on the road. Even with the overcast bleakness, the Northern Rockies patched here and there with spruce, held a certain beauty. My loneliness was triggered for lack of having someone beside me to share this beauty with. My duffle didn't count. Nevertheless, the car diligently climbed mountains and descended into winding river valleys for nearly seven hours when, approaching the top of a rise, the little-green-VW-bug-that-could suddenly decided, it could no longer. With sputtered deceleration and unresponsive to any pressure applied to the gas pedal, the car convulsed to a dead stop. On the left the cliffside dropped dramatically to the river below, to the right a mountain stretched skyward with me balanced somewhere in between. I checked the time. It was noon.

I turned the key in the ignition. The starter reacted as usual, but no response from the engine. After several tries, and to save the battery and avoid any further damage, I got out and moved behind the car. I opened the engine compartment checking oil level, fan belt, anything that made sense to me. I could see nothing wrong and headed back to the car.

The rain, having stopped hours before, left behind a dampness that clung to skin and clothes like an unexpected frost. I shut the door to keep any remaining warmth from escaping and thumbed through the owner's manual for some indication of what to do next. Nothing made sense as I read. My fingers panicked through the manual, nearly mutilating scores of pages at a time as they jumped between the index and corresponding information. How could I search for a solution when I didn't know what was wrong? My lack of mechanical knowledge was beyond frustrating. The frustration quickly turned to fear.

I began to panic and considered abandoning my car and walking into the forest. I imagined the car and all my belongings joining the wrecked and demolished vehicles I had seen along the way. Cars, campers, trucks, useless castoffs at the bottom of a ravine bordering the highway; an unmanaged junkyard of rusting metal, pushed over the edge by owners suffering serious mechanical or spiritual breakdowns.

Out of the corner of my eye I noticed something low to the ground approaching from the sloping terrain on my right. I checked both side and rearview mirrors. There was no one behind me. In fact, there had been no one behind me or in front of me for more than two hundred miles. No trucks. No cars. No one.

I sat up straight, dropping the savaged owner's manual between my legs and clutched the wheel with both hands. My eyes surveyed the car's perimeter, left side, down and beyond the sloping hood, right side. The small rear window prevented an accurate surveillance of what could possibly be lurking behind the car. I managed to release my grip on the steering wheel long enough to lock both doors when from around the rear driver's side bumper it appeared, moving slowly along the edge of the car. It looked to be a large dog, maybe a German shepherd, but the color was off, too gray and thick with fur, the beginning of a winter coat. And then it hit me. W-O-L-F. Sweat broke out across my brow.

I watched as the animal sniffed a circle around the car. It hesitated as if in deep thought, then climbed the embankment stopping only once to make eye contact with me before taking advantage of the mountainside's camouflage and disappeared from view.

It was becoming all too clear now that being eaten by a hitchhiker was not the only fear I had to face on this journey. There were other ways to be devoured on this desolate roadway, and I needed to keep an open mind to an unexpected fate. I began to contemplate what would happen if no one came along to save me. This was not Prokofiev's orchestrated tale of Peter and the Wolf. No hunters' tympani salvoed my rescue. Peter's heroic march would not trumpet a win for me that day. I thought to myself, how dramatic it would be to be eaten alive by wolves. I was sure he'd come back, yellow eyes vibrant against dark fur, and bring all his famished friends, lolling tongues salivating with anticipation. Maybe

I'd even freeze to death during the night and not have to worry about the beasts at all.

I never had an automotive breakdown at the summit of a mountain before, let alone one in the Yukon. Hell, I had never had a breakdown with a car before at anytime, anywhere, except for my previous car, my first car, a worn-out Sunbeam Minx that had a tragic starter which required positioning a long metal rod on just the right spot and tapping it with a hammer to get it to respond. I didn't have to look at a manual to figure out what was wrong. The maneuver nearly always worked until in frustration one time, I hammered the rod straight through the brittle starter casing, hence a brand-new VW beetle.

When hope for rescue seemed at its lowest, something, a sound, more like a rumble, distant and muddled, interrupted my nihilistic internal dialogue. Looking out my side mirror I caught view of a large rig barreling toward me, sending up a low-level dampened cloud of gravel as it approached. The rig began to slow, down shifting and reversing the direction of its dust wake forward and between us.

The truck pulled up behind me and stopped. The cab door opened and out jumped the trucker, someone I imagined to be in his late twenties or early thirties, a Stetson, denim shirt and jeans and an open red flannel-lined waxed canvas coat. He looked familiar, perhaps a muleteer from the roadhouse at Milepost 462.

I leaped from the car and walked back to greet him. He sensed my excitement, rather relief in seeing him. I explained to him what had happened.

"Do me a favor," he said. "Try starting the car."

I jumped back in the car and turned the ignition expecting nothing, but somehow it started.

"Now, try driving it a bit."

The car sputtered forward, a few feet at a time. After it traveled about ten feet, he signaled for me to stop and to turn off the engine.

"Let's have a look." He nodded toward the engine.

Opening the back, he checked the motor and fiddled with the distributor cap. Titling his hat and smirking, he walked back to his truck and rummaged through a medium sized toolbox. He returned with a small wire brush and a piece of emery paper. Kneeling in front of the engine compartment, he fiddled with the distributor cap. He began to sand and brush each spark plug, removing, as best he could, a combination of carbon and oil build-up that was preventing the sparks from igniting and setting the pistons in motion.

Pulling a rag from his pants pocket and wiping his hands he then eased into the driver's seat and turned the key while putting slight pressure on the accelerator. The car stammered to life. He climbed out and left it running.

"Well, you may be all right for a while, perhaps as far as Whitehorse; that's about another 150 miles. But your spark plugs are worn out and no damn good and because of this you'll need a new distributor cap."

"Wow, thanks for discovering what's wrong.»

"There's a service station in Teslin 'bout forty miles up ahead. They might be able to help. Get gas, too. Remember this, when you fill up your tank, don't turn off the engine, it might not start again. You'll most likely keep a decent speed on flat stretches, and you'll buck up mountains, downhill you'll be fine. Be careful."

I grabbed my wallet and offered him some money, but he raised his hand signaling it wasn't necessary or expected, an Alcan good deed. A legitimate smile replaced his earlier smirk. It meant everything to me. It warmed me, dispelling any earlier chill I was feeling from him. I returned to the car and drove off. He followed for a while, and soon gained enough speed to pass me, air horn voicing two short blasts goodbye.

Perhaps I was a bit green to attempt this solo journey and despite being blown off the road somewhere in Saskatchewan and stranded on a mountain for a time in the Yukon wilderness, I was going to be okay. When things looked bleakest, there was always someone, at least so far, who came along to lift me out of my panic, to provide the assistance I needed or a promise for help up ahead, whether that was a man driving an old rusted blue pickup, a prairie crossroads mechanic, or a truck driver in the middle of nowhere. These strangers helped and saw me back on my way, usually with a smile by the end of our encounter. The isolation I was experiencing, while significant when I was alone in my car, was in fact, tempered by these experiences, these highway good Samaritans. Looking back over my life, I see how this has always been the case. When in danger, lost or in need, someone shows up, a guide, a confidant or a stranger who changes my life for the better.

I drove on, taking sometimes forty-five minutes to climb a hill, jerking forward at five to ten miles an hour, holding my breath, and exhaling on the downhill descent as I made better time. A good while later I pulled into the gas station in Teslin, rattled from the car's jerking about and the unevenness of the Alcan's pitted gravel roadway. I remembered not to turn off the engine. A mechanic came out to fill the tank. I told him about my predicament. He couldn't help. He'd have to order parts and it would take a few days before he'd have them. It was best to push forward to Whitehorse.

150 miles and six hours later the low-level static from the radio began to mingle with garbled sounds of a song not quite fixed on the dial. Civilization, I thought, the first radio reception picked up after two days and hundreds of miles of nothing. I fiddled with the tuner and brought in a relatively strong signal as Crosby, Stills, Nash and Young's *Our House* made its way out of the strident speaker, filling the car's cabin with the familiar; an ordinary moment somehow bringing me to tears. I loved that song; it was one of my favorites. I let the melody and lyric wrap around me in a much-needed musical hug.

It was well after dark when my bug crawled into Whitehorse. Checking into the Travelodge at Second and Wood Streets, I exchanged hellos with the clerk. She asked how my day had been. I gave a *Reader's Digest* version of the breakdown. She nodded, her

show of sympathy well-worn from having heard similar tales of woe and worse at least weekly from ill-fortuned drivers coming off the highway. I asked the clerk my all-important question, the only one on my mind.

"Maybe you can help me here. Is there a well-equipped garage that handles mechanical problems, even on a Volkswagen?"

"Sure thing, there's a garage within walking distance of the hotel," she looked out the window and pointed down Wood Street. She grabbed a paper placemat with an illustrated street map of Whitehorse and penciled in the route. "It's closed now but opens first thing in the morning. They'll fix you up."

I thanked her and made my way to my room. Exhausted, but also in need of a decent meal, I wandered the streets around the hotel until I found a tavern serving meals. Peeking through the thermal plate glass windows from the sidewalk, the crowd appeared to be a mix of people, families, and a group of men straddling stools along a bar. It looked inviting, safe and I'd keep my eyes from wandering where I'd draw unwanted attention. I didn't want a repeat of me checking out the men as I had the night before at Milepost 462. I got a table and ordered a burger and fries and downed two bottles of beer without incident.

When I got back to the Travelodge, I sat down at the desk and wrote a letter to Herbie detailing the day's adventures, how my car broke down, the trucker who happened along as if by magic to get me up and running again, and how very lost I felt after breaking down at the top of a mountain along with the fact that "I almost walked into the forest out of hysteria." After writing Herbie, I capped off the night noting in my journal that "at times I felt as though all was over for me. The Yukon is beautiful but unimagi-nable when alone and in trouble."

The next morning, I brought the car in for its much-needed repairs and had the mechanic do a full tune up in addition replacing points and plugs and anything else that the car might require to get me to Anchorage without further delay. It took

entire day, which meant a second night in Whitehorse. I'd still meet the deadline for reporting to my alternative service assignment on November 1, but I'd have to drive the remainder of the trip without interruption—no breakdowns, no wolves, no stopping, except for gas.

I used my time while my car was being worked on to do laundry and explore the river front, which was just a block away from the Travelodge. It was lined with abandoned sternwheeler steamships, decaying relics of the Klondike Gold Rush. I wrote another letter to Herbie, which had now become a daily habit, and for supper that evening, I returned to the tavern where I ate the night before. While there, I ran into an older couple who I'd already met earlier at the Travelodge. The man was from Allentown, small world, and they were headed to Fairbanks. The brief encounter reminded me of how far away I was from home and how lonely I felt at that moment. I departed Whitehorse early the next morning.

* * *

WHITEHORSE TO THE ALASKA BORDER WAS A 300-MILE DRIVE. A hundred miles after crossing back into the United States, I passed through Tetlin Junction before arriving in Tok, the first place since crossing the border to feel like somebody lived there. I took the Tok Cut-off, the 139-mile highway, including a short stretch of the Richardson Highway, that would take me to the junction with the Glenn Highway, and the final 189-mile leg into Anchorage. I was going to do this 700-plus mile trip in one long day.

The ride brought me into rugged landscapes, through mountain passes, alongside a glacier crawling back into the mountains and a drive-by sighting of a lone wolverine prowling at the edge of the roadway. It was well beyond anything I could have imagined; with the sun setting around 3:30 p.m. halfway between Tok and Anchorage, the beauty, even in darkness, was a surprising reward as I neared the end of my journey.

I began to feel a sense of relief as I drove on into the night, having fought for months to be classified as a conscientious objector, seeking support from family and friends as I maneuvered through the appeals process permitted by the Selective Service. Now having survived the long ordeal I was ready to begin my required alternative service working with Alaska Children's Services. I'd arrive in time to start work the next morning.

A Change in Plans

MY TWO-YEAR MANDATORY SERVICE TO THE COUNTRY began with a job with Alaska Children's Services as a relief counselor at Anchorage Children's Christian Home, a receiving home that served as an emergency shelter for kids in immediate need of a safe place to stay. My weekend shift started late Friday afternoons, and I was on duty through Sunday evenings. Along with another relief counselor, a woman from Vermont, we relieved the permanent house parents, a young couple from Colorado, so that they could have a couple days off each week. The children who temporarily made this building home ranged in age from newborns to older teens, abandoned and seeking sanctuary from families gone wrong, dead, or missing. Alaska Children's Services included this shelter, along with a series of group homes and a more secure residential center for troubled youth scattered throughout the city and as far north as Wasilla. The entire operation was formed through an unlikely alliance of three religious organizations—the American Baptists, Methodists, and Evangelical Lutherans. While they all worked together for a common cause, each sect claimed command of a specific group

home, residential center, or emergency shelter, placing missionaries at each site to oversee the work and promote the respective
denomination's doctrines.

It was nearly 8:00 p.m. when I came to a stop, letting the engine
have its well-deserved rest. Legs stiff from the long drive, I got out
of the car and faced Anchorage Children's Christian Home, managed by the American Baptists. I was in a subdivision of reasonably
sized houses, a nice neighborhood. Situated at the end of an unfinished street, a cul-de-sac where spindly black spruce trees served
as a natural barrier preventing further development, for now. The
house was redwood-sided, rough-hewn and lacked any painted
trim. Next door was an identical house which functioned as a girls
group home. From the outside there was no indication that these
structures were institutions serving children in crisis. They looked
just like any other homes in the neighborhood.

Overcast skies and a damp thirty degrees encouraged me to get
inside the house to warm up. I knocked on the door closest to the
driveway. There was no response. I peered through the window
next to the door. It took a few seconds for my eyes to adjust to the
interior darkness in the house, no shadows or movement detected,
nobody home. I began to wonder if I had misread my directions
when I was pulled back toward the entryway by a diminutive ghost
named Ernie. His hand extended from the sheet that covered him
and grabbed mine as he led me into the house where other ghosts
and ghouls roamed and bounced to Bobby Pickett's *Monster Mash*.
I had completely forgotten that it was Halloween and the kids and
house parents clearly had not.

Everyone seemed interested in my arrival, the new relief counselor to handle weekend duties. Thirteen-year-old ghost, Ernie,
proudly introduced me to the rest of the family. I soon learned
from reading the reports and daily journals, that he had made it to
the shelter after his mother accused him of killing his father who
had drowned in a river while drunk. Ernie had a fascination with
French fries, which he would wave around like tiny swords during

those meals when they were served. The resident social worker accused him of having a penis fixation. I thought he was just fooling around, but what did I know.

The work at the receiving home was hard. Unlike the boys at the boarding school where I had worked during college, and who had come from mostly well-to-do and upper-middle class families, these kids had come to us through such terrible circumstances that it was a struggle for me at times to keep a safe emotional distance so as not to become too sad or upset by their current situations. If I felt helpless in trying to help them, it would only diminish my ability to be effective in doing my job. There was a certain hopelessness that hung over the house and could be seen in each child as they waited to be placed in foster or residential care. Recently vacated beds were quickly filled by what seemed to be an endless stream of damaged kids. And while I tried to rise above it, for the benefit of the children in my care, that hopelessness began to seep inside me, too. It penetrated my being and clung to me like a deceptive fog trailing from my feet no matter where I went, becoming thicker and slowing me down as my time at the shelter went on. If this was how I would be feeling during my two years of service, then I'd begin to understand what the draft board meant when they said that there should be an element of hardship associated with being a conscientious objector.

Originally when I was hired, I was assigned to two sites, three days a week as a relief cottage group counselor at the Lutheran Youth Center in Wasilla, a residential treatment center for ten boys; and two days a week at Anchorage Children's Christian Home, a receiving home for kids in crisis until they could be placed in a more permanent facility. The combined positions paid $400 a month and included room and board. The salary was way higher than what I would have been making as a first-year music teacher back home, but then the cost of living in Anchorage was two to three times higher, too. My permanent residence would be in Wasilla. I was asked to begin in Anchorage first, as that was where

I was scheduled to work on weekends, and November 1, the day my local draft board ordered me to report for civilian duty, was on a Sunday. This also made it easier for me to meet with the Alaska Children's Services' director of program services, Ken Fallon, on Monday morning, before heading up to Wasilla.

Except, that didn't happen. On Monday morning I drove up to Alaska Children's Services main office on Abbott Road. Ken met with me and said there had been a change in my duties and that he had no way of letting me know while I was en route to Alaska. I'd now only be working weekends at the emergency shelter in Anchorage, just two days a week. I asked him how that might impact my alternative service requirement, always worried that my local draft board was monitoring my every move as a way to rescind my conscientious objector status and send me off to Vietnam or prison. He assured me that all the draft board would need to know was that I was employed by the agency that the draft board had approved for my service. Then he added that in a couple of weeks he'd have me begin covering at other sites as needed, probably at the girls group home next door to the receiving home so I'd still be full time. So, for now I'd be at the receiving home and next door at a girls group home. However, he informed me that room and board was no longer available. There was no suitable space at the emergency shelter to house additional staff. He kept my salary at $400 a month but added an additional $50 as a housing compensation. I spent my first and second nights on a cot in the shelter's small office.

On Sunday I picked up the Anchorage Daily News and learned that Jim Morrison had been fined $500 and sentenced to six months in prison for indecent exposure and profanity. Besides his music and lyrics, it was his onstage antics and misbehavior, his rebelliousness that attracted me to him. The article pointed out that he was going to appeal the court's decision. I then scanned the classified ads looking for a furnished apartment and spent part of the day scouting out the city to get a feel for its neighborhoods. I lucked out right away and found what I was looking for.

The apartment was in the city, near Cook Inlet, with mountain views and close to shops and restaurants. If the next two years required me to be here in Alaska, working with these kids in need, then at least I'd found a place to call home during my alternative service stint. I wasn't in the Army carrying a gun or living in a tent at the edge of the jungle or in jail or exiled in Canada, as I'd feared would happen had I not been granted conscientious objector status. I could do this, complete my service, meet my obligation to the country and return home all in good time.

Sunrise, Sunset

ON NOVEMBER 2, I MOVED INTO A ONE-BEDROOM furnished apartment at $210 a month, including utilities, on M Street edging a bluff overlooking Cook Inlet. The bluff defined what remained after the land now below it had dropped significantly during the massive '64 quake. Measuring an astounding 9.2 on the Richter scale, the most powerful ever recorded in North America, I could still see the scarred remnants the quake left behind in a few neighborhood structures and in the eyes of those who lived here. This elevated location provided a magnificent view across Knik Arm. Looking out from my porch I could glimpse the reclining Sleeping Lady, Mt. Susitna, which resembled a pink-hued silhouette of a giant reclining woman in afternoon sunlight.

In early morning, from the same porch, I would watch the arriving black swarms of C5A Galaxies accented by the dawn's first light and sounding like rolling thunder, carry home their cargoes of daily dead and severely wounded, tallied each night in numbers on the evening news. Each time I saw these monstrous flying beasts, feeling the sky shutter on their descent or ascent, their massive shadows rippling over Knik Arm, I thought about being a CO, of why I was doing what I had to do. I was never angry with those who chose otherwise or who involuntarily found themselves the hunter or the hunted in rice paddies and Agent Orange-doused jungles, whose passage home or going off to war depended on these very planes.

In the dead of night and on the other side of town, commercial jetliners commandeered for service by the government appeared as if push-pinned to the night sky as each plane waited its turn to be untacked and flutter down to expectant gates at Anchorage International. Sleep-deprived recruits fresh from Lower 48 boot-camps clambered down ramps to board busses to Elmendorf Air Force Base in darkness, virgin troops to replenish the now empty flying hearses for the return to Vietnam.

* * *

NOT QUITE A YEAR LATER, ON SEPTEMBER 27, 1971, I would ride past these enormous planes sleeping in darkness along runways and beside massive hangars. As unlikely as it seemed, I was on my way to one of these hangars, decked out in full presidential pomp, all the regalia befitting the arrival of a world dignitary, in this instance, Hirohito, the Emperor of Japan, the first Japanese member of the Imperial Family to ever set foot on foreign soil. The man who was responsible for igniting the war in the Pacific during World War II and sanctioning the attack on Pearl Harbor. He was on his way to visit leaders in seven European countries, stopping at Elmendorf to refuel after an almost nine-hour flight from Tokyo and to briefly exchange greetings with Richard M. Nixon.

My invitation was not a personal one arriving on official White House stationary and requiring an RSVP, but rather a general group offering afforded to churches and other organizations in the area, perhaps to make sure there'd be a crowd to greet the Emperor and President.

Nixon had arrived earlier in the day, primarily to meet with his former Secretary of the Interior, Walter J. Hickel. Hickel wanted to mend fences with the President after the two had had a falling out after the former Alaska governor had criticized Nixon and was subsequently fired; but primarily he was attempting to leverage Nixon's support in opening the vast North Slope oil fields for drilling.

For days I fretted over the chance to be there in person. Should I go, or shouldn't I? As a conscientious objector and someone who had publicly opposed our military presence in Vietnam, I wondered whether the Secret Service would even let me stand among several hundred people in a hangar the size of Rhode Island. But like my draft board, who never once checked up on me during my entire stay in Alaska, the Secret Service also didn't seem to care whether I was there or not. For that matter, I don't remember being screened or having to maneuver through any security checkpoints. In the end I was merely an insignificant bystander tagging along with Chuck Eddy and his wife, Mary, two people who would enter my life in June 1971. We moved into the hangar and joined others standing in the Alaska cold and waited.

So here I was, in person, watching as Hirohito was met by a waiting Nixon. A president I was losing patience with due to the never-ending war and an upcoming five-megaton nuclear warhead test on Amchitka Island in the Aleutians. This test, nicknamed, *Cannikin*, was to be the last of three to be detonated there. This final blast, once it was detonated, raised Amchitka's ground surface by roughly eighteen inches, generating rockslides and seriously disturbing the island's volcanic base. The blast registered 6.8 on the Richter scale. The series of nuclear tests prompted environmental activists to form the Don't Make a Wave Committee, which would soon become the non-violent protest group, Greenpeace.

The Emperor was scheduled to arrive at 10:45 p.m. At 10:30 p.m., the large bay doors slid across their tracks like theater curtains, the pitch-black darkness outside seemed at first to suck the light right out of the hangar. It grew colder around us. The crescendoing whine of jet engines reverberated through the immense structure. Then, coming into view was a Japan Airlines DC-8. The plane was taxiing right into the hangar and coming to a stop with its tail still exposed to the outside beyond the immense doors. A red carpeted staircase was rolled into place, the plane's forward hatch opened, and Emperor Hirohito and Empress Nagako made their way down the steps and greeted President Nixon and First Lady Pat. Two drummers kicked in with a thunderous drum roll on large, eagle-clad snare drums reminiscent of the American Revolution as the President and Emperor made their way along the red carpet to a small, raised platform. The U. S. Army Herald Trumpeters' long horns snapped in place against waiting lips and blared a fanfare in Japanese mode, then Four Ruffles and Flourishes, brass gleaming under the hangar's vapor lamps. A twenty-one-gun salute cann-oned off the hangar walls followed by the playing of the national anthems of both countries. The pomp and circumstance reduced me to tears like it always did, touching something deep inside me, not just patriotism, but something more, something about com-munity. It was like the reaction I got when a high school marching band would pass by me at a small town Fourth of July parade or when bagpipes played at a funeral. Something about rituals, music and people coming together got me every time.

Both men made remarks, tributes to each other and our respective countries. It was all too brief as they were escorted to a waiting limousine. As the scene dissolved into the blackness out-side the hangar, we saw the bullet-proofed limousine speed off. Nixon and Hirohito would spend 35 minutes at a nearby house for conversation and a photo op before the Emperor boarded his flight to Copenhagen.

Thanksgiving

I WROTE HERBIE ON WEDNESDAY, NOVEMBER 25, 1970, just a few weeks into my alternative service assignment that, "Thanksgiving will be hard away from home . . . But Christmas will be the worse of the two—I will be working. I do not wish to be alone. I may even spend the night at the receiving home. Oh, well, there are better things to think about other than loneliness."

The next day, which I assumed would be less than a special holiday away from my family turned out to be one of the best Thanksgivings ever.

A group of us from Alaska Children's Services were invited to spend the day at one of the administrator's homes. We had staff and kids from a couple of the group homes, many of us away from our families both here in Alaska and the Lower 48. For more than a few of us, it was not our choice. We went ice skating from midmorning to around three that afternoon. The house backed onto a large lake, and now that it had completely frozen over, it became an extension of the backyard. It was a large gathering with the administrator's family, his neighbors, and the rest of us.

We stopped a couple times for hot chocolate and to warm up a bit. On one break someone had put on the 1959 recording of Beethoven's *Ninth Symphony* conducted by Bruno Walter with the Columbia Symphony Orchestra and Westminster Symphonic Choir. A great recording, which sent me into reveries of being back East, Westminster Choir College and home. The Ninth was a particular favorite of mine ever since last spring when we performed it with Leopold Stokowski and the American Symphony at Carnegie Hall.

While skating I met an 8-year-old neighbor's kid who asked if I wanted to take a ride with him on his snow machine. There were a few snow machines idling at the shore along with motorcycles that would regularly scoot off with their riders laughing and whooping across the frozen surface of the lake. The ride was exhilarating, and I marveled at my young chauffeur's skill at handling the machine. It was a great ride and when we returned to the house, I thanked my diminutive driver and told him how much fun I had riding with him.

At 4:00 we went inside, tossing our winter gear in a guest bedroom, and joined the family for their Thanksgiving feast. There were so many of us that the meal needed to be served buffet style. We'd never fit around our host's dining table. We grabbed plates, silverware and napkins and loaded our plates with strips of Alaskan salmon candy, slices of roast caribou, reindeer sausage and foods I was more familiar with back home—turkey, sweet potatoes, and the rest.

After the meal, we said our goodbyes and headed back to the girls group home to play board games and then went tobogganing until after 10:00 p.m. The whole day was great fun, and I was deeply thankful to have been included in this wonderful celebration.

Riding on my Thanksgiving high, the next morning I went off with Lucille, the lead counselor at the girls group home, and we each bought a pair of cross-country skis, poles, boots, and wax to keep the base of the skis slick. The winter in Alaska would not keep me trapped inside under an electric blanket. I was going to make the most of the next two years.

This Is What I Signed Up For

ONE OF OUR LITTLE SQUIRRELS WAS IN BAD SHAPE. A boy visiting Ernie hit the animal with a rock, or so I was told. I think it was a cover story to shift the blame from another resident, Bob. Bob had been given a slingshot for Christmas by the receiving home's house parents, Karen and Ben. I think Ben picked it out, maybe not the best choice for a kid in crisis.

Bob seemed scared and wouldn't tell me about the accident, probably for fear of losing his slingshot. He liked hunting and had a fascination with killing animals. He had already been warned that if one animal was ever harmed near the receiving home, he'd lose his toy. Then he started to cry. The squirrel lay there paralyzed, I think its back had been broken. It couldn't move. Bob wanted to take the squirrel to his room. I took it to the ASPCA instead.

* * *

I HAD BEEN WORKING AT TWO SITES, Anchorage Children's Christian Home, and next door at the girls group home. The numbers at the girls group home had dropped to three residents, and with a staff of four, it wasn't financially sound to have all of us there. Ken Fallon, my top boss at Alaska Children's Services, asked me to take on an assignment at one of the Jesse Lee Home's residential treatment cottages for 12- and 13-year-old boys for the next month or until they'd get back to having six residents at the girls group home.

The Jesse Lee Home was a Methodist mission orphanage founded in 1890 on Unalaska, an island in the Aleutians. The orphanage served hundreds of Aleut children until the mid-1920s when it was relocated to Seward in a move to broaden its mission in serving more children. When the 1964 earthquake struck on March 27, the Jesse Lee Home, because it was situated on top of a hill, escaped the tsunami that hit the town below. Nevertheless, it still suffered serious damage to its buildings. The United Methodist Women, the denomination's official organization for women, then purchased twenty-five acres of land on the outskirts of Anchorage to serve as the new site for the Jesse Lee Home. Construction began shortly thereafter, and the Jesse Lee Home reopened its doors in 1966. The new complex included an administration building for Alaska Children's Services, four residential cottages, each with a large kitchen, a common room and cookie cutter dorm-style bedrooms down a long hallway. It felt clinical, antiseptic, and cold, very different from the receiving and group homes in the neighborhood I'd been working.

As a relief counselor filling in at Alaska Children's Services various sites around the city, I was required to attend, along with the rest of the staff, regularly scheduled in-service training sessions to learn about and practice current methods and strategies for working with our diverse population of children. We had all been instructed in what at the time was called a *holding session*. A holding session was employed when a child became so physically and/or emotionally upset that they would become a danger to themselves and others nearby. It involved physically restraining and becoming one with the child by wrapping your arms and legs around them until they had regained a sense of calm and well-being and no longer posed a threat. The practice is now considered controversial because of restraint related injuries and deaths. At the time, it was seen as therapeutic with little attention paid to any resulting physical or emotional harm to the child. The practice should have been left to the professional therapists on staff to administer rather than the barely trained COs, volunteers and missionaries who staffed the group homes and residential cottages.

Holding sessions were hard work and required both physical and emotional stamina. When the holdee was in crisis it seemed like their physical strength increased tenfold and the anger and hostility directed toward the holder was intense. While I had not previously needed to use the technique at either the emergency receiving shelter or girls group home, I was told that it would be more frequently needed with the boys I would soon be working with at the residential treatment cottage at the Jesse Lee Home. First, however, I needed to spend a few days observing the counselor who I'd be replacing for the month.

* * *

THE WINTER MONTHS CAN SEEM LONGER than the days allotted to each during the Alaskan winter. January 1971 seemed even longer working with the eight boys at the residential treatment cottage, and it was only the fifth day of the month. The boys went back to school on Monday following the Christmas-New Year's break. On Tuesday, six of them had decided to cut school and once the school bus had dropped them off at the schoolhouse door that morning, they took off. They then conveniently returned to campus at dismissal time and jumped back on their school bus for the return ride home at the end of the day. I think they thought we would be none the wiser of their antics if we saw them getting off the bus at the end of the day, but the school had called reporting them as no shows that morning.

The incident triggered a mandatory house meeting, even for the two who didn't skip. The house meeting was really a group therapy session to address cutting school and the behaviors leading up to and after the incident. The house seemed settled by the end of the meeting.

Later, though, right after supper, four of the six who had played hooky decided to take off again and were still missing at 11:30 p.m. It appeared they ran off together, which is better than being out there alone. The temperature was 40° or so most of the day, which was higher than normal for that time of the year, but nights, regardless of daytime highs, could be brutal.

One of the boys, David, who had skipped school with the others, but hadn't run off that night, asked the house mother if he could watch television.

"No, David, you can't watch TV tonight because you cut school today."

In response, he then dumped his glass of Kool-Aid all over the kitchen floor.

"Fucker," David yelled back at the house mother. She called the other counselor on duty, the man I'd be replacing. He was a big guy, an ex-cop who was getting his degree in physical education in three weeks. He wanted to be a gym teacher.

I had watched all of this happen but hadn't officially started at the cottage yet, not until the next Sunday, so was asked to merely observe, to not get involved.

"David, clean up your mess right now," the ex-cop ordered.

"No, pig!"

The counselor then retrieved a mop and industrial mop bucket, the kind on wheels, from the hall utility closet. He kicked it toward the boy. As it skidded toward David, water splashed over the sides adding to the mess that was already on the floor.

"I'm not doing it."

What I saw next was beyond disturbing. The counselor grabbed David and forced him down on his knees, hard.

"You're hurting me," David cried out.

"Clean up your mess," the ex-cop bellowed. Still holding the kid by the scruff of his neck, the man pushed the kid's face to the floor and rubbed his nose in the spilt Kool-Aid. He then grabbed David by the waist picking him up and flipping him upside down. He then proceeded to mop up the sugary red liquid with David's long blond hair.

When he had finished mopping the floor with the kid, he released him. David, however, wasn't quite finished. He got up, defiantly filled another glass with Kool-Aid, went over to the cottage supervisor's office door and spilled the contents on the floor for a second time. The counselor returned volley by grabbing the kid again and dipping him headfirst into the new spill. This led to a 45-minute *holding session.*

I didn't like the physical force used to address David's behavior. It was unnecessary, I thought. There had to be a better way to deal with this. Even after being used as a mop, and the counselor telling David that because he indeed had been used as a mop that he had cleaned up his own mess, the kid refused to admit it.

* * *

ONCE I OFFICIALLY BEGAN WORKING AT THE COTTAGE, it didn't take long before I had to put my training into practice. I had a kid, Sam, in crisis and he was completely out of control. I had been having a holding session with him for at least 30 minutes. When I thought he was ready, I let him up to see if he could handle himself. I was exhausted and I realized I had made a mistake; he wasn't ready to be on his own just yet. Once he stood up, he pulled a 12-inch spike out of his desk drawer. I don't know what it was doing in his room, or how I hadn't seen it before. He came at me with it, intending to injure me. I couldn't get close enough to grab the spike from his hand, he had a long reach and clearly wanted me out of his room. We moved around each other until I got in front of the door leading out into the hall, at least it appeared like he wanted me to get to the door. I asked him if he wanted me to leave and he nodded. Sam wasn't the kind of kid who ever harmed himself by cutting or exhibiting any signs of suicidal ideation. From what I could tell, he was in no danger of hurting himself. I opened the door and got out of the room as he came at me. Somehow, he had also picked up a pair of scissors in his other hand. I closed and secured the door as he slammed into it from the other side.

After some time had passed, I went to do a bed check, to make sure everyone was getting ready for lights out. I noticed that Sam's door was slightly ajar, and he had the light on. He was on the bed. I went back in his room and asked him if he was feeling better. He said he was. We talked briefly about what had happened and mentioned that what he was doing was dangerous. He agreed. I told him I was taking the spike and scissors for safekeeping. He nodded. I asked him if he would go to sleep now. He said yes. All was quiet.

* * *

A COUPLE DAYS LATER, AGAIN AROUND BEDTIME, I had another holding session with a 14-year-old Aleut boy, Boris. I had to hold him for 45 minutes. These sessions were extremely difficult and painful for both me and the kid I was trying to help. But mostly it's heartbreaking to see kids get like this. While I was holding him, he spat at me thirteen times, don't know why I was keeping count. I never blinked once during the ordeal. When it was over and I'd had a chance to wash up, I almost broke down and cried, but I held it together. Boris was so angry, wouldn't go to bed and threatened anyone who got near him, me included, by swinging his belt around his head, the metal buckle fanning out and away from him.

I was never angry or lost my temper with any of these kids or their actions, even after being spat on. Boris had even scratched my hand so badly with his fingernails, digging deeply into the soft fleshy area between my right thumb and index finger, that I still have the scars to prove it.

A few days later, Ken Fallon came over to me and put his arm around my shoulders. He asked me how I liked working with the boys. I said I liked it fine. Maybe I'd be asked to work with these boys all the time and that, indeed, would be fine by me. If not, I'd do whatever was needed to make a difference in these kids' lives.

Jimmy Sunnyboy

Bird reflections think
they are fish flocking
across the river's surface

Slicing through capped waves
as if cutting through clouds
until they reach the shore
and become as shadows

Earthbound and bouncing
up the bank's muddy rise
crossing mounds, reeds,
and winging east
and out of site while

Otters spin in eddied bliss
and ladder up the brink
as if climbing playground slides
to slip down greasy gutters worn slick
from furry backs and bellies.

A shirtless Yup'ik boy
waits on the bank
'til sparks ignite and tiny eyes
invite and joins the game of slip and slide.

Some question still if this is true,
that otters play with boys along
the Andreafsky River shore
but Jimmy did and told me so
and tells me how he laughs
at night and dreams
of otters in his sleep that stay with him
until he wakes.

In this shelter far away
from his St. Mary's village home
he finds me in the common room,
a question resting on his lips,
and asks me if the otters miss
a boy like him
as much as he does them.

The Message

January 23, 1971

Dear Herb,
    I called a person last Thursday to give a message to the
church that I had to cancel choir rehearsal . . .

The thing is, I don't remember working with a church so soon
after I arrived in Anchorage or having a choir for that matter. In
rereading my letters to Herbie, I see that I wrote to him about starting a choir shortly after I arrived. My only thinking now is that it
might have been a Methodist Church, St. John's, as I had befriended
a minster who had a church that was somehow connected to
Alaska Children's Services. The United Methodist Church, which
managed the Jesse Lee Home, was one of three ministries, along
with the American Baptists and Evangelical Lutherans, that joined
forces in unifying the various group homes, shelters, and residential treatment centers in Alaska.

    . . . Well, by the time it got to the church it was all mixed
up—a poor speller got a hold of it. It read—

"Don Proffit called
there will be no
queer practice tonite
he's strated"
It should have read, no choir practice, he's <u>stranded</u>.
I wonder if she meant "gone straight."
(Or was this something more intentional, more sinister.)

Love
Buzzy

Not Interested

I HAD JUST FINISHED UP MY WEEKEND SHIFT at Anchorage Children's Christian Home, Friday afternoon through Sunday evening. My coworker was a woman from Plainfield, Vermont. Our responsibilities ranged from cooking meals and doing laundry to providing activities for the children currently living at the emergency shelter. I would also drive kids to church on Sunday mornings and when the weather cooperated, would take a group to a park for a bit of outside recreation. We had a two-month-old with us this weekend, so I also changed her diapers and bathed her whenever she needed, something I never learned how to do at Westminster Choir College. At least I could sing her a lullaby better than I could change a diaper.

It was a quiet weekend, no emergencies, or unusual crises among the kids or from the outside. We were always on guard should a dysfunctional parent, guardian, or an estranged family member—after being separated, sometimes forcibly, from their child—learned where their kid was staying and show up and cause a scene.

As my shift was ending, I decided to let the regular house parents, Karen and Ben, a young married couple from Colorado, know that I was leaving and would see them both next Friday. They had just returned from a weekend away. Ben was also a conscientious objector. I tried befriending him several times since starting my alternative service at the receiving home back in November, but always felt snubbed by him whenever I made the effort.

They had a small suite of rooms, a private apartment, at the back of the house, which included a master bedroom, bath, and small living room. The suite felt like a neat and tidy home with pictures of family and friends on the walls, a television set, comfy chair and sofa, a plush area rug, coffee table and well-stocked bookcase. Their rooms were a serious contrast to the rest of the house with its dorm-like bedrooms on the second floor, an all-purpose room with a large raised carpeted platform with industrial fabric-clad bolsters and beanbag chairs for lounging, boxes of toys and children's books, and coats, scarfs, boots, and assorted kids' sports equipment spilling out of the mudroom which led to the garage. The kitchen was huge. All of it seemed stark and cold, no kids' drawings on the refrigerator, no pictures of their families placed on tables or shelves. No child stayed for long, I think there was an unspoken rule that said we don't want the children in our charge to feel too comfortable here, not to treat it like home as they would either be reunited with their families soon, which rarely ever happened, or they'd be placed in foster care or in one of Alaska Children's Services collection of residential group homes as soon as the legal paperwork was filed and an open bed became available.

I knocked on the door to let the couple know I was ready to head back to my apartment. I heard muffled talking through the door and then, more clearly, Ben's voice.

"The door's unlocked, just come in and have a seat."

As I entered the living room, I heard the bedroom door click shut. The conversation behind the door continued, still muffled and a bit stilted. Were they having a fight? When the door to the bedroom reopened, Ben came out wearing his bathrobe, which was untied and hanging open, revealing a skimpy pair of red bikini briefs.

At first, I wondered if I had interrupted an intimate moment between the two of them until I remembered the muffled conversation behind the door.

"Is everything okay? I can give you a call in the morning to go over what took place over the weekend if that would be better. I don't want to bother you two."

"Nope, everything's fine and your being here is not a bother. Have a seat." Ben gestured toward the sofa, which was small, more like a love seat for two.

I took a seat and Ben came around the coffee table and sat next to me, which made for a slightly uncomfortable situation, for me anyway. I didn't need to be exposed to his open robe and tiny briefs. I was uncomfortable and started talking about the weekend's highs and lows, how individual kids were doing, and anything else he might need to know for Monday morning. Anything to keep him engaged in conversation about our residents and me from looking at how he was dressed, or rather how he was *not* dressed.

Ben didn't seem to care all that much in what I was telling him, but instead reached over to grab a large book of professionally taken photographs. It looked like an expensive coffee table book that you'd purposely put out on display when you were trying to impress special guests at an exclusive dinner party, but I soon felt uneasy once I saw the cover. He placed the book on the coffee table and flipped it open to a random page.

"Have you seen this book?" Excitement was in his voice and eyes.

The thing was, I had seen the book before. I even wrote Herb back on November 5, just a few days after arriving in Anchorage, that I was impressed with the couple's poetry collection and noticed the book. I knew it didn't belong to Karen. I also wrote Herb that Ben was a bit distant and seemed to treat me coldly whenever I was around. There was something about him that worried me that had nothing to do with my gaydar. He had majored in drama in college and played the piano, so minimally, I thought with having the arts in common, he'd warm up to me more. Tonight, however, his normally cold shoulder was anything but.

It was an art photography book geared toward a specific audience who might appreciate the aesthetic exhibited within its matte finished pages. Its contents nothing more than hundreds of photos of nude boys in what some might say to be *artful* poses. Boys on swings by a brook, boys idly fishing on a riverbank, boys stretched out on divans and fur rugs, all with innocent expressions and slightly suggestive gazes for page after page, an expensive bound portfolio now masquerading as a flirtatious come on.

I had seen a similar book, or it might have been the same one, while having cocktails one Sunday in Manhattan at some church organist's apartment on the upper Westside. I'd tag along into New York City sometimes with a Westminster Choir College organ student. We'd catch the evensong service at St. Thomas on Fifth Avenue and then join the organist and a few others from St. John the Divine or St. Bart's for a couple of stiff drinks, usually gin martinis, which would knock me off my feet, and supper at a nearby Chinese restaurant before heading back to Princeton.

I was not amused in what was happening or seemingly about to take place with Ben. I felt trapped between his wanting me to respond every time he picked out a specific boy he wanted me to look at and having to sit beside his nearly naked body as he made an exaggerated effort to expose more skin each time he stretched to turn to a new page. I was not interested in wasting my time on some sordid dalliance with this man.

I was upset that his wife was in the next room and that he was behaving in this manner. I still saw marriage as a sacred bond between two people and even the slightest sign of infidelity would upset me. I thought the whole thing inappropriate and awkwardly tried to tell him so.

"Ben, I've got to go. I came in to discuss the weekend with the kids, but I can come back tomorrow to fill you in. I'm not looking for anything else. Sorry."

He seemed indifferent to my awkward response and simply shrugged. Maybe they had an arrangement, that their marriage was merely a cover. This was not something I wanted to be a part of, I had Herbie to think about.

I said goodnight and left. When I saw Ben next, it was as if the attempted act of seduction never took place. His aloofness had returned. Even if I was craving a physical embrace, some much needed affection or more from another person, this was not how I wanted it to take place, while someone waited alone and listened behind a closed bedroom door. I would not be the one to come between these two people who I worked with and cared about or commit an act of momentary passion that could prove harmful while a houseful of displaced children were tucked in their beds in the rooms above.

I didn't bring up the incident again to him or anyone else for that matter. I did learn a few months later that Ben had left the Anchorage Children's Christian Home after an incident took place between him and one of the adolescent boys in his charge. I was angered about the incident and disappointed with Ben's behavior and lack of control. That he could put one of our kids already in crisis in further jeopardy was unforgivable.

I'm Not Karl!

I SOMEHOW FELL INTO THE COMPANY OF AN ODD GROUP of men. Their oddity only came to light when I found myself hanging with them in the basement apartment of a plump middle-aged man who resembled a character out of a Dickens' novel, the kind you should most likely avoid; not like a Fagin, but more like a Bumble or Sowerberry. Housing in Anchorage was expensive and to find someplace cheap meant settling for shared, cramped and often dismal spaces, like this windowless basement room in someone's private home. He wore a cape . . . all the time. When he pulled it closed around his tumescent middle you could see the sloppy spattered remnants of a recent meal's bolus that had dribbled down the garment's front. The stains reminded me of the food-soiled commoners or scholars gowns worn by Princeton students in a dining hall I stumbled into by accident one evening while wandering the campus in the late sixties. His two companions, now that I look back, were perhaps more concerning, in that they never seemed to question the Capeman's ideas or actions. They reminded me of henchmen following their boss's orders in carrying out some shady scheme.

I must have met this crew a few months after arriving in Alaska when I was still working in emergency shelters and adolescent group homes for kids in crisis, my Selective Service alternative work assignment, before my time working with the people of St. Mary's Episcopal Church in June 1971. I say this because, once I found myself involved with the church, my circle of friends seemed to improve. More than likely, I came to know these men after attending a community theater performance, which they were either acting in or patrons of, maybe it was in January. They seemed to take an interest in me for some reason—I don't remember if I was being flirtatious or merely looking lost—after the performance had ended and while attending a small meet-and-greet with the cast and crew. We were chatting about the Anchorage theater scene when the Capeman suggested we continue our conversation in a more private setting as the building we were in was about to close for the night. I followed them back to the Capeman's apartment. I missed that part of my life and thought that becoming active in community theater again would be good for me, something to help remedy the long darkness of the Alaskan winter and the emotional stress I'd accumulate each day while working at one of the city's emergency shelters or group homes. Maybe befriending these three would give me a better chance at joining the company. But once I got to the Capeman's apartment, things turned weird.

These three believed they were reincarnated friends and relatives of Beethoven and divinely brought together to finish writing his *Tenth Symphony*, a work that Beethoven had begun composing prior to his death but never completed. When they were talking to me about this project in the Capeman's cluttered one-room, dungeon-like basement apartment, they mumbled something about the *Curse of the Ninth*. The long-forgotten rumor was most likely spread by Gustav Mahler about how a handful of Romantic era composers had died once they had finished writing a ninth symphony. Turns out it was all fabricated by Mahler. He was obsessed with the idea and even seemed to believe it. After he composed his eighth symphony and before starting his ninth, Mahler decided to write a symphonic-like work for two singers and orchestra, *Das Lied von der Erde*, thinking he'd be able to outsmart the curse. The opus was to be a decoy to distract the curse. When it was completed, he then wrote his ninth symphony. He died anyway while composing his tenth.

At any rate, the trio exposed their outrageous plot to me around a small wobbly coffee table surrounded by stacks of books, piles of classical records, discarded clothes, and a random assortment of junk, all while sipping glasses of cheap sherry and nibbling on stale Ritz crackers. The Capeman said they'd been waiting for me to join them as the missing link they needed to realize a finished Beethoven's *Tenth Symphony*. I had never met these three before, so found it unfathomable that they'd been waiting specifically for me. I think anyone that they would have encountered that night in the theater's lobby, and who had the misfortune of following them home, would have heard the same tale. They thought I was the reincarnated spirit of Karl van Beethoven, the composer's nephew, who Beethoven fought over in a contentious custody battle with his brother's widow. I knew the story, having read the account in a Beethoven biography while a student at Westminster Choir College.

Although my mother occasionally talked about being reincarnated, I'm not sure I was ready to believe that line of thinking just yet. I do recall during my early twenties, however, of having a recurring dream, a nightmare really, of living in Vienna in the mid-1840s and waking up at the exact moment I was about to cross a street and be crushed to death by a quick-paced horse-drawn streetcar. I didn't think I was Karl in that dream. He died in 1851 from liver disease not from a tram accident.

With Karl supposedly residing in my body, the trio felt they'd have the power to reach out to the maestro himself, who would then feed the needed musical notes to the Capeman, or rather me as the musician in the room, from the great beyond, capturing fragments of leitmotifs in what sounded to me as an unlikely Ouija-like dictation process.

One part of me, the small crazy part, was flattered, even though I wondered why Ludwig himself hadn't opted to invade my body. The rest of me was scared out of my mind as I scanned the room for an exit, hoping desperately that the only door in the room was unlocked. I eyed the door with its concealed narrow staircase hiding behind it and waited for a lull in the conversation to make my escape. The lull arrived and I offered my thanks to the Capeman and his little friends for their hospitality and a no thanks to the offer of helping them, stating strongly, "I am not Karl!," and bolted out the door, up the stairs and into the bleak midwinter's night and freedom.

As I drove back to my apartment, I heard my mother's familiar warning about strangers in a strange land and how she worried that I'd be cannibalized when I least expected it. I considered finding an exorcist to cleanse my soul, but instead decided that maybe community theater wasn't what I needed in my life right then.

Closet Under the Stairs

I CONTINUED AS A RELIEF COUNSELOR at Anchorage Children's Christian Home and filling in when needed at other Alaska Children's Services' sites from when I arrived on November 1. I was meeting my obligation as a conscientious objector, doing what I believed to be a good job and making a positive difference in the lives of the children I was serving, or so I thought. On a Friday afternoon in June, now nearly eight months into my two-year alternative service assignment, I showed up for the beginning of my shift. The social worker on site, Mary Lee Nicholson, a matter-of-fact woman but someone who cared deeply about children and their needs, asked me to join her in the small common office at the back of the house.

"Don, I need to speak with you about your work here," her conversation began.

"Okay."

"A few things, really."

"Okay."

"First of all, I've noticed that you're not keeping up with your log entries, which need to be made at the end of your shifts on

Sunday nights, or anytime there is an incident with a resident. When you comment on a child or a situation in the house, it lacks details." Mary Lee produced the logbook to point out the differences between my entries and those of the other counselors. She further stressed how important these entries were when working with city and state children and family services agencies or the Bureau of Indian Affairs.

"Then, recently you took the older residents to the 4th Avenue Theater two Saturdays in a row to see *M*A*S*H*. And I don't think the film was appropriate for our residents and there are other activities for the whole house that the money spent on tickets could have been used for."

The conversation, so far, was one sided, but I really liked that film, and how it depicted another side of war as nurses and surgeons tended to the wounded and dying while also engaging in antics to somehow distract themselves from the war's carnage. While it took place during the Korean War, I saw it as taking place in Vietnam. I thought that the teens in my charge enjoyed it, too, but maybe I was wrong, maybe I failed to recognize the needs of the kids I was working with. I remembered that the film was rated R with no one under the age of seventeen admitted without a parent or guardian. I saw myself as their guardian, which in a temporary way I was, but just so I could get them through the theater doors. I thought little about the film's moderate amounts of sex, gore and intense scenes that might upset some of the kids. Then the conversation took a disastrous turn.

"I think you're suffering, a little bit crazy right now." I couldn't believe she used the word "crazy" to describe, in fact, what I might have been feeling at this moment. "And I don't think you continuing here is what's best for our residents or you for that matter."

I sat there stunned. The criticism burned. No one had told me that my log comments were less than adequate. Writing in the log was not my favorite task and to this day I dislike filling out reports. It's an unwelcome chore. Maybe there were times I failed to make an entry on a specific child or two when there didn't seem to be anything that warranted a written response. Once Mary Lee had pointed out the stark difference between my entries and the rest of the staff, I could see how weak mine were. If I had received some feedback along the way about needing to improve my work ethic, I certainly would have tried to remedy any concerns others might have had.

She suggested I get counseling. All I could think about was the fact that I had a nice apartment and had begun to make friends. How was I going to pay for everything? Where was I going to live? And then it hit me, how would I be able to complete my two years as a CO?

"Don?"

"Yes."

"Are you all right?" I wasn't but was not about to admit that to her, so I said nothing, kept my head down while she continued. I was angry and wanted to reject her talk of counseling as soon as she said it. There was nothing wrong with me as far as I was concerned. Looking back, I can see that I needed help. Maybe I was just showing up for work, marking time until my shift was over. I wonder now if there were cues or hints from the people I worked with that I somehow missed, or refused to admit to hearing or seeing, not wanting to be seen as a failure or to jeopardize my conscientious objector status when I had just sixteen months to go. I couldn't start over; I wouldn't go back until I met my obligation to the country.

I felt the office close in around me, the spindly black spruce trees outside the window seemed to distance themselves. The opposite effect of what I witnessed looking through this same window on my first meeting with Mary Lee back in November, when I noticed the trees appearing to roll toward the house, followed by a loud cracking sound and the desk and chairs jumping up and slamming back down onto the floor. At that time Mary Lee asked if that was my first tremor, just a slight earthquake she said, nothing to worry about.

"I realize that a lot of things are going on in your head right now. I know you're thinking about paying rent and how you'll manage your alternative service requirement." I looked up, finally, and faced her.

"Yes, that's a problem."

Mary Lee had a solution, though, not perfect, but would turn out to be better than I thought would happen as it unfolded over the months ahead. She had asked Ken Fallon, the director of program services at Alaska Children's Services, to help her brainstorm some options as a way for me to continue doing my alternative service without alerting my local draft board about losing this job. A job that I was required to complete as a CO, a job that I thought I was being successful at until Mary Lee pointed out my less than adequate log entries and that I needed to better understand and meet the needs of the children in my care, not drag them off to a Saturday matinee of *M*A*S*H* that I only found entertaining. I may have been in a depressive state during those first few months after arriving in Alaska and just didn't recognize it; the loneliness and isolation creating a barrier to being fully engaged in my work at the receiving shelter. Maybe that's the crazy that Mary Lee was trying to convey to me.

Ken had arranged for me to meet with Father Chuck Eddy, a former marine turned priest, at St. Mary's Episcopal Church in Anchorage. I had heard that name before and realized that this was the priest that Father Packard Okie in Emmaus suggested I connect with before I left for Alaska. A deal had been worked out that Father Eddy would provide me with a place to stay, some work, and weekly counseling, which he would personally do himself. His name sounded familiar, but I couldn't yet place where I'd heard it before. She also said that, while not the same salary, the church could pay a small stipend that would be funneled through Alaska Children's Services so that my salary would continue to show that I was employed by the agency that the Selective Service understood to be my official employer. Additionally, Alaska Children's Services would continue to submit any reports required in documenting my time as a CO.

It seemed like Mary Lee and others had done a lot of work on my behalf prior to this meeting, yet there was a part of me that didn't like the fact that people were talking about me behind my back. I tried to process what was happening, and maybe deep down appreciated that people cared, even if I could not express it at that moment. Another part of me, however, saw this plan as a conspiracy against the government, this deal I was given; a form of money laundering where the church funneled money to the children's agency and then passed it on to me, all to keep me safe and allow me to continue meeting my obligation to Uncle Sam. It was all so cleverly creative and a bit subversive— I could deal with that.

There was another reality at play that had nothing to do with what was happening to me here in Alaska. The reality was that local draft boards were overwhelmed during this period of the war, so much so that monitoring conscientious objectors, once we had been dispatched on our civilian duty assignments, was often overlooked, or neglected all together.

I could tell that my conversation with Mary Lee had come to an end, but she seemed to have something else she wanted to add.

"I'd like you to write this down and keep it, it might be helpful, maybe not today, but maybe someday later on."

I grabbed a pencil and a scrap of paper from the desk. When I was ready, Mary Lee shared a line of verse, words that seemed more like a directive than poetry, about looking beyond my own selfish needs and turning my attention toward those with little power, with no one to protect them and therefore needed my loving and care for them to survive.

"Do you have it?"

"Yes."

"These words were written by John Berryman." I wrote down his name, too.

Before walking away from our meeting with Berryman's words written on a slip of paper as my only severance, knowing somehow that the words were meant to inspire me in some way, Mary Lee dug into her wallet and handed me a hundred-dollar bill.

"Here, take this, just in case you need it. It's not a loan so I don't expect you to pay me back, just pass it on to someone else in your life who may be in need. You'll know when."

I left the office placing the slip of paper in my shirt pocket and the hundred-dollar bill in my wallet and went back to the quiet of my apartment to sort through all that had happened. I sat on my couch and took the scrap of paper out of my shirt pocket and reread the words, "Take up, outside your blocked selves, some small thing that is moving & wants to keep on moving & needs, therefore, . . . your loving." I carefully placed the piece of paper in my wallet and carried it around with me and moving it along to each new wallet I'd purchase over the years until it eventually turned yellow and became brittle with age, coming apart at the folds and disappearing a piece at a time. As I got older, Berryman's words made more sense to me, especially as I began my career as a teacher. Later I discovered that the quote was from Berryman's poem, *Death Ballad*, about two teenagers, Jo and Tyson, who had been institutionalized in a psychiatric ward after both had attempted suicide. Over time I finally settled on a meaning that worked for me and that was that it wasn't about me, it was about others, and finding compassion and empathy for others beyond my own tendency toward selfishness. I still think about Berryman's words and how, if I could've just gotten outside of my self-centered and *blocked* self, my struggle with being gay and a conscientious objector during that period of my life, that perhaps I could have had a greater impact on the children in my charge—children that just wanted to overcome their hardships, hardships that had been placed on them by others, and therefore needed my *loving*.

And unlike Berryman's words on the slip of paper, which later disintegrated to the point that I had to write it down in a journal to preserve them, I continued to pass along the monetary gift, whether in coin or deed, to others. I only hope that in paying her gift forward, that it was done with a similar sense of grace and without diminishing the one in need or expecting it ever to be returned as she had done for me.

* * *

IN THE DOWNWARD SPIRAL THAT FOLLOWED losing my job at Anchorage Children's Christian Home and not fully accepting Mary Lee's assessment of my job performance, I asked Ken Fallon, who was, after all, the person who hired me, if he would do a favor for me. I wanted to see my employee file, thinking one of my references from Westminster Choir College had said something about me being gay, which might indicate, in Mary Lee's eyes, that I was unfit to work with children, *a little bit crazy*. I wondered if anything in my file might have influenced Mary Lee's decision. I had never read through the file to see what my references said about me. For some reason I either assumed or received a message that recently graduated students using the college's job placement service should not be privy to the contents of their files. It was something about confidentiality and protecting the integrity of the reference. Even though I asked specific professors to write reference letters for me, people I trusted, I was sure there was something written in their letters that provoked all this, that it couldn't be my fault or behavior or who I was.

* * *

LOOKING BACK, I WONDERED IF THERE WAS SOMETHING placed in my job placement file that had to do with my attempt to move back on campus in January of my senior year. It was right after I decided to leave my job at the boarding school where I worked during college and where I had just completed my senior student teaching requirement. I wanted to spend spring semester living on campus.

I went to meet with the dean of students to request a dorm room. He referred me to the college chaplain who wanted to talk with me first, which I thought strange. He indicated that there were no rooms available right now and that it would be best to find a room off campus. Off campus housing usually meant a student-filled boarding house or a room in a private home. I scouted around Princeton for a place, not quite sure why I was doing this as I knew of vacant dorm rooms at the college. I found one room that was in a stately white village colonial off Nassau Street, across from the university, a longer walk to the Choir College. When I called my parents for the rent, they questioned why I was doing this when there were rooms available at Westminster. My parents were willing to file suit against the college for denying me a room.

Returning to the chaplain's office, I restated my need for a room on campus and that I knew there were beds available, even a single room with no need for a roommate.

"Well, Donald . . ."

"You can call me Buzz, please."

"Well, Buzz," followed by some hemming and hawing on his part, "our concern is that your situation may not mesh well living with the other men in the dorm."

"And what situation is that?" Then it dawned on me, it was because I was gay. A term I started using more frequently, coming into greater usage in the mid-sixties and the one more widely accepted by others like myself to refer to a homosexual. I wanted to let him know that there were many more like me in this music school, living on campus, and that, truth be told, a larger percentage than most colleges. I kept that part to myself.

"We understand that you're a homo . . ."

"Gay?" I cut him off. "Please understand that I'm not here to bother anyone else or cause any problems for the college. I keep to myself for the most part. I'd like a room, in a dorm, not off campus as you suggested. You can place me in a single with no roommate if that's your concern. My parents have retained a lawyer should that be required in order to get a room." I don't think my parents had done that yet, but at that point it seemed like the right thing to say and saying so seemed to change the outcome of our conversation.

"Alright, I'll check availability. It will probably be in North Hall. Give me an hour."

I checked my student mailbox around noon and discovered an envelope. Inside was a note indicating a room number on the third floor of North Hall and a key. I made my way to the dorm, climbed the three flights of stairs, and unlocked my new room. There was a stripped bed against the right wall and to my surprise, sitting on the bed to the left was my new roommate, a sophomore who I'd seen on campus. A decent guy, a Southern Baptist, who prayed for me each night, sitting there in his bed, a reading lamp illuminating his well-worn bible. We rarely spoke during that spring. I think I scared him because I was gay.

For a small college there seemed to be a disproportionate number of gay students enrolled. Closets were still in fashion, especially on campus, mostly for keeping our secret lives secret, and friends were careful in not outing each other outside of our circle. While we were a secular institution, the college had its beginnings as a choir at Westminster Presbyterian Church in Dayton, Ohio in the early 1920s, so the school was well-rooted in the Protestant traditions that rose out of the Reformation. Unlike today, where LGBTQ+ acceptance is more readily embraced in the Presbyterian Church, that was not the case in 1970.

* * *

THE NEXT MOMENT I WAS USHERED INTO IN A SMALL ROOM off the main office of Alaska Children's Services, and seeing my file on the table, began pouring through the documents. All my references were glowing, maybe except for one person who stated that I was extremely shy, and once I could overcome that, I'd make a wonderful music teacher. There was no mention of the dorm incident senior year where the college chaplain felt that for me as a gay man, he'd prefer it if I lived off campus. I assumed his stance was taken to protect what he thought was the sanctity of the Christian sensibilities of the college. Both relieved that there was nothing about me being gay and annoyed that I was outed for my shyness, I thanked the director for his help, returned to my apartment on M Street and thought hard about taking my next steps in all of this.

Another thing dawned on me once I got into my apartment and had a chance to process what had happened, reading through those recommendations in my file indicated that I had the needed talent and skills to be a successful teacher, to work with children. While working in a group home wasn't the same thing, my time working at the boarding school and being a successful student teacher demonstrated that I could work with kids and that they seemed to genuinely like me. Maybe Mary Lee was right, that I needed a little to time get myself back on track.

I didn't know it then, but in a few months, I would return to work in good standing at an adolescent boys group home in an Anchorage subdivision, working as a relief counselor for Alice Aiken, in her mid-fifties, a polio survivor and former Idaho potato farmer who ventured north in search for something meaningful to do after her husband died unexpectedly. Alice and I had been good friends since I arrived in Alaska. Chuck Eddy became my emotional and spiritual guide during my remaining time as a conscientious objector and Alice served as the down to earth and straightforward coach I needed to help me become an effective counselor. I'd become a regular in the group home kitchen, even if I was off duty, drinking coffee to excess, until my knees quaked and tingled (wobbled even when I got up to walk) from too much caffeine. I admit I loved that feeling, a bit of a wired high and with the bonus that Alice made a great cup of coffee. She even offered her RV, a new purchase for her escape back to Idaho and unknown places when she thought the time was right, parked in the group home's driveway as an occasional place to sleep, a welcome reprieve from what would become my cramped living space at St. Mary's.

Now without a job, I had no choice but to give up my downtown apartment and seek refuge in what was an unexpected place. Through an offer from Father Chuck Eddy, I took up very public lodging under the stairs in a sloped ceiling storage closet in the basement of St. Mary's Episcopal Church—my sanctuary and the means for maintaining my conscientious objector status and fulfilling my alternative service obligation. The offer included the responsibilities of serving as church organist and choir director. I wasn't an organist, at best I had skill as a functional pianist, so I treated the church organ like a piano, careful not to step on the pedals by accident after a hymn, anthem, or prelude. I had done that on occasion, sending a discordant blast reverberating through the church from the choir loft above and garnering scowls from the congregants and a confused glance from Father Eddy standing alone at the altar. I also was charged with setting up coffee for Sunday services, assisting teachers at the Creative Playschool, an early childhood center which ran during the week, and managing the homeless shelter that the church ran during the short Alaskan summer, all for which I was paid around $110 monthly, a far cry from the $450 a month I got from Alaska Children's Services. I even mentioned in a letter to Herbie that it wasn't that bad, that the cut in salary meant I'd have just enough to get by on and I'd be paying less war tax. I told him I was becoming a struggling artist. All in all, it worked out just fine, because in a few months I'd also have a small income from relief counseling at one of the boys group homes, the one Alice Aiken managed.

My narrow space, like living inside a right triangle, was filled almost completely by a single cot, which I would later switch out for a waterbed—maybe not my best decision. I didn't need a frame for the bed as when it was filled with water it expanded snuggly from wall to wall in the closet. Because the cement slab floor was so cold during most of the year, I now needed to buy a heater for it, a thin 3-foot rectangular envelope of sealed vinyl film which concealed the heating element within. It was like having a heating pad under the bed and it kept me from catching hypothermia or freezing to death during the winter nights.

I squeezed out room for my stereo record player and somehow managed a makeshift bookcase to hold my treasured volumes of Gide, Rimbaud, *The Whole Earth Catalog*, *Be Here Now*, and *Winnie the Pooh*, to name a few. I hung my clothes on the coat racks set up in the small hallway across from my closet and between the two restrooms. My wardrobe became public knowledge within a week.

Just outside my closet was the church's parish hall, which was usually reserved for Sunday school classes, refreshments after services and evening vestry meetings and bible study. Late at night, when I had the entire church to myself, this modified basement underneath the sanctuary became my observatory to the winter nights' displays. A bank of windows looked out over a bluff to the Chugach Range east of Anchorage and the sky above. Here I would watch the Northern Lights fill the sky so brightly that I'd stand at the nearest window for hours marveling at its beauty. The lights were eerie and magical, and whether they were slowly appearing orbs, familiar flowing curtains, or glowing rods streaming upwards until they vanished deep into the sky, the moment they'd come into view, was the moment when I'd become centered and calm.

Inuit tribes tell different stories about the lights. Some legends tell of the aurora as a realm of heaven offering peaceful respite to individuals who had endured a violent end. Others describe the changing lights as reflections of the spirits of the dead or a bridge to the afterlife illuminated by hosts of torch-carrying spirits. While some would argue that whistling at the phenomena would force it too low to the earth, bringing the perpetrator bad luck or death, others saw it as a way to whisper to the spirits. Whether whistling was seen as taboo or a way to connect with a departed loved one, I wasn't concerned. As a child in northern Massachusetts, we lived far enough north that on a cold clear night, my mother would wake me up to see the lights when they were present, and we would bundle up and go outside together and whistle to see if we could make the aurora dance. So sometimes, when the church was empty and the evening sky held the promise for more than just stars, I'd find myself whistling alone by a window bleeding cold air, waiting for the lights to appear so I could make them dance again.

* * *

JUNE 13, 1971
DEAR HERB,

IT HAS BEEN DIFFICULT IN REPLYING TO YOUR LAST LETTERS. I HAVE STARTED FOUR SO FAR AND HAVE BEEN DISAPPOINTED IN EACH.

DRAFT BUSINESS IS OK. NO ONE NEEDS TO KNOW. THE PEOPLE WITH THE CHILDREN'S AGENCY HAVE ALL NEEDED INFO IN CASE THE DRAFT SHOULD GET SNOOPY. THEY WILL BE TOLD I AM STILL WITH THE AGENCY. NEAT.

I AM TAKING A CUT IN SALARY FROM $8,400 TO AROUND $3,000, WHICH ISN'T A HELL OF A LOT TO LIVE ON IN ALASKA. BUT SOMEHOW, I LIKE THE IDEA OF HAVING JUST ENOUGH TO GET BY. NO EXTRA WAR TAXES. SO NOW THE STRUGGLING ARTIST I'M BECOMING.

I HAVE READ AND RE-READ YOUR FIRST LETTER (PHILOSOPHICAL ONE) MANY TIMES. I FIND IT ALL QUITE GOOD. I WOULD LIKE TO KNOW YOUR FEELINGS NOW THAT YOU ARE IN OHIO AND HAVE MADE THE MOVE. I WANT TO KNOW IF YOU HAVE ALTERED ANY OF YOUR THINKING.

RIGHT NOW, I WANT TO BE A SHEPHERD ON A MOUNTAINSIDE. I THINK I AM MOVING IN A MORE NATURE ORIENTED TREND RIGHT NOW. BUT

TODAY I DID WRITE A SHORT CHORAL PIECE AND
FIND THAT SINCE LEAVING THE OTHER JOB MY
MIND HAS SHOWN A LITTLE MORE CREATIVITY
THAN USUAL. I WILL HAVE SOMETHING SPECIAL
FOR YOU IN THE NEXT COUPLE WEEKS IF I DO NOT
LOSE INTEREST IN THE PROJECT. NOW I'LL RAMBLE.

IN LIFE, TOTAL LIFE, THERE IS NO BEGINNING
OR END. WE MOVE LIKE SCATTERED CLOUDS
FOEVER. IT SEEMS TO ME THAT OUR ONLY
REALITY FOR NOW LIES IN OUR BEING AWARE
THAT WE SOMEHOW EXIST. I CAN NOT SAY
ANYMORE NOW OR I'LL GET FUCKED UP. I CAN'T
AFFORD THAT NOW BECAUSE I'M ALONE IN THIS
CHURCH. WELL NOT REALLY ALONE. THERE IS A
VERY BRIGHT GLOW IN THIS CHURCH THAT HAS
VISITED ME ON VARIOUS TIMES. IT IS VERY WARM
AND EXTREMELY LOVING. IT FIRST VISITED ME
ON MY SECOND NIGHT HERE AT THE CHURCH. I
WAS FEELING KIND OF SCARED BEING ALONE IN
A CHURCH AND SLEEPING THERE WHEN THIS
GLOW APPEARED TO ME IN MY CLOSET. IT WAS
AS IF IT HAD COME TO COMFORT ME. IT IS SO
BEAUTIFUL THAT EVEN NOW THERE ARE TEARS
IN MY EYES FROM THINKING ABOUT IT. IT VISITS
REGULARLY AND HAS AT TIMES GOT ME OUT OF
SLEEP. PERHAPS IT IS PART OF ME. PERHAPS IT IS
YOU. NEVERTHELESS, IT DOES EXIST. BUT A GLOW
HAS BEEN SEEN IN THIS CHURCH BEFORE BY THE
PRIEST'S WIFE. SHE DESCRIBES IT AS A VERY WARM
FEELING TOO. PERHAPS THIS IS WHY I'M HERE
AND HAVE BEEN THINKING HOW EVERYTHING
SEEMED TO BE PULLING ME TO THIS CHURCH
A FEW MONTHS AGO. PERHAPS ALL MY LIFE.
MAYBE I SHOULD TRY SENDING IT TO YOU. I'LL

TRY TONIGHT. THINK BACK TO SOMETIME IN THE
EARLY MORNING HOURS OF MONDAY THE 14th OF
JUNE WHICH IS THE TIME AS I WRITE THIS LATE
SUNDAY NIGHT. I'LL TRY VERY HARD. IN FACT, I'LL
START NOW.

I MUST FIND MORE TIME TO COMMENT ON
MORE OF YOUR LETTER. I FOLLOW ALL YOU HAVE
SAID SO FAR. LOOK INTO NATURE A LITTLE MORE.

IF MY MIND CONTINUES ON CERTAIN PATHS, I
MAY RETURN MY CO CLASSIFICATION, BUT SHALL
ROAM FREELY AS I WISH AND BE WITH YOU.

I HAVE NO VACATION UNTIL MAYBE JANUARY
72. SUMMER IS BEAUTIFUL HERE. IT IS STILL LIGHT
OUT AND MUST BE CLOSE TO MIDNIGHT. I AM
ONLY HOPING THAT YOU CAN MAKE IT HERE
SOMETIME EVEN IN THE FALL IF YOU HAVE TO.

I WILL PREPARE TO WRITE ABOUT ART AND
FREEDOM LATER. I WOULD IMAGINE WE ARE
SUPERMEN.

LOVE
BUZZY

Getting Acquainted

It DIDN'T TAKE ANY TIME FOR FATHER EDDY to get me involved with the church. By mid-June during a gloomy spell of rainy days shortly after I moved into the closet, Father Eddy asked me to join him and his wife, Mary, for dinner at a parishioner's house in Eagle River, twenty-five miles or so north of Anchorage. The family had two sons, one had been Mr. Alaska a couple years back and had arms the likes I had never seen before. I thought maybe a bit overbuilt, and not my type. Their other son, who I didn't meet that night, was twenty-one.

The mother, a Newfoundlander, had prepared a fantastic meal, very British—roast beef and Yorkshire pudding. It was an unexpected (and delicious) feast for a Wednesday night. Once dinner was done and we were headed back to the living room, the mother pulled me aside and asked me to join her in the kitchen. I thought maybe I was being enlisted to help with the dishes, which I would have gladly done but that wasn't the case.

When we were alone beside the stacks of dinner plates, pots, and pans, she spoke to me about her older son, the one who wasn't present for tonight's meal. She said how he had wanted to be a conscientious objector, had been or was about to be drafted. Similar to my struggle in obtaining a 1-O classification, it sounded like he was facing some of the same barriers in convincing his local board of his reasons for becoming a CO. Now, she said, he was no longer around. She'd not seen him in months and had no idea where he went. I didn't know what to say, but thought, *what a fucking waste.* I reached over to her and hugged her, a long, deep hug. We were both crying when we separated from each other and then we did the dishes.

On the drive back to St. Mary's, Father Eddy asked me how I felt the evening went. I told him about my kitchen conversation. Father Eddy already knew, having been briefed on our talk by the mother before we left. He said she had really opened to me, and that she never talks about it at all with anyone. I thought, maybe it had to do with me being a CO and was glad she felt she could take me into her confidence.

* * *

IT WAS THE LONGEST DAY OF THE YEAR and when I crawled out of the closet, I expected to be greeted by sunshine, but all I could see were low hanging clouds cutting off the tops of mountains along the Chugach Range, a sharp contrast from the night before.

Father Eddy, Chuck, had asked me to join him at a healing service as part of my orientation to all things Episcopalian. I had no idea that the Episcopal Church went in for things like that. I always thought that the laying on of hands was a ritual solely practiced by Pentecostal Christians.

When it was my turn to receive the laying on of hands, I walked up to the altar and was greeted by two priests. They had me sit on a chair then placed their hands on my shoulders and the top of my head. It was amazing. I could feel something happening and could also see the white glow I had seen before at St. Mary's. It was all very clear, both in my mind and through my eyes. I felt renewed, lifted in a way I hadn't experienced before.

* * *

I WONDERED, AFTER THE APPARITION AT ST. MARY'S, and during the laying on of hands, if what I was experiencing was like the glowing orb that had visited and passed through me when I was a teenager in Illinois. On its first appearance, I thought it might have been the beam of a gyrating Mars Light from an approaching eastbound Rock Island train. These locomotive headlamps moved in a figure eight pattern to serve as a warning to motorists at railroad crossings, passengers waiting at stations, and animals, both farm and wild, roaming Illinois pastures at night. I thought that maybe the lamp's swiveling beam made its way into my bedroom as it approached our town, Tinley Park; but the glow that was before me was constant, not subject to the blinking interference a locomotive light beam would suffer as it sputtered behind houses, barns, and a roller rink as it made its way toward Chicago. My orb was the shape of a softball made of fog, a bluish-gray glow like that of a black and white television screen after the National Anthem had played at station sign-off late at night. It seemed to float in over last season's few remaining dead cornstalks left in the fields behind our house and then straight through my bedroom window. It entered through the soles of my feet, pausing in my throat, and using my voice box to utter a gravelly "ah," and then exiting from my mouth. It had done this three times over one week at the end of January. Its last visit witnessed by my parents from their bedroom at the end of the hall. They never doubted my visions or questioned whether I was fabricating these ghostlike sightings just for seeking their attention.

These orbs of light would occasionally visit me. Only one time did I feel a sense of dread when one of these mysteries appeared without warning. It was in Herbie's attic bedroom in Toms River while we were college freshmen. I was standing between the cot his mother had set up for me and Herbie's bed when a forward leaning web of light made its presence known to us. The humanoid apparition seemed to be made up of a collection of balloon animals molded out of flexible, glowing florescent tubes. Herb saw it first as it moved through the closed bedroom door. It approached us and passed through my body before leaving through the wall at the corner of the room. I felt a buzz, like a mild electrical shock, and then my body temperature dropped. I vocalized the familiar, sustained "ah" sound that sometimes accompanied these events. Herb said the left side of his body, the side closet to where I stood, tingled and felt icy cold as the apparition passed between us. This one felt different from the others I had experienced. This one felt evil, very dark and menacing.

All in all, my ghosts trailed me until my mother's death when I was twenty-seven years old. I thought for a while that she was a medium and attracted these spirits. Or imagined we shared a power to conjure up these phenomena. Then they vanished for good, or so it seems, on the day that she died.

* * *

AFTER ATTENDING ANOTHER SERVICE THAT NIGHT, maybe for the solstice, I joined Chuck and his family and took a ride up into the mountains outside of Anchorage and parked in a gravelly spot that afforded a view. The clouds that hung around for most of the day had departed. The view was beautiful, and we could see McKinley, now called Denali, some 250 miles away, the evening light illuminating the peak in pink—what a delight after a long and emotionally draining winter.

In the days that followed, Chuck had me do a deep dive into sacred music. I read an article in the *Episcopalian* on sacred music and the new Episcopal Hymnal. It was by Lee Hastings Bristol. Dr. Bristol had been Westminster Choir College's president when I started there as a freshman in 1966; I enjoyed his presence while a student at the Choir College. He was a character, though. I remember him in top hat and tails sitting at the concert grand regaling us with Gilbert and Sullivan patter songs. He even donned a monocle for these *très gay soirées musicales*.

I felt good about what I was learning and that I had a place here at the church, doing something that I cared about. It helped ease some of the *Sturm und Drang* I felt at times as a CO; times when my anger would rise when talking or thinking about the war or the unfairness of the draft or when someone would question my patriotism or being verbally assaulted or physically threatened for being a conscientious objector.

The Poor Wind

THE CHURCH SAT ON A SLIGHT bluff looking out and over a valley toward the Chugach Mountains, the range that bordered Anchorage on the east. The wind encircled the structure, constantly spinning and taking on visible form whenever it rained and snowed. The only change was in its direction, clockwise or counterclockwise, in your face or at your back, depending on the time of day or year. It was always there.

While the wind made itself known outside of the church, I began to make my presence known on the inside. As the resident organist and choir director, I was also charged with devising a project to engage the older teens and young adults. I had already made connections with the local folk musicians in the Anchorage area. Many of them assisted at Sunday services, especially during folk masses, a regular occurrence at St. Mary's in the early '70s. My love of folk music and the fact I had a banjo, provided the motivation for what would become a regular gathering of local musicians, the church's youth group, and the community. We began working on the coffee house concept in September 1971, gearing up for an official opening in October.

The youth group wasn't big, but it did include a few others not directly associated with the church, including the son of Ken Fallon, my old boss at Alaska Children's Services. Ken had asked me to look after him, to help him get involved with other older teens and young adults in a meaningful endeavor. We liked the idea of opening a coffee house, a monthly evening of song, with cinnamon-laced Tang warmed in one of the large coffee urns, Russian Tea we called it. Add in candlelight, homemade cookies, roasted sunflower seeds and a rotating roster of Anchorage's best folk singers and you had the makings for a great night out.

The coffee house occupied the church parish hall beneath the sanctuary. Not quite a basement as it had a bank of windows running along the side of the building at ground level, the other wall built deep into the bluff. The space was unequally divided into three sections. At the far end was a good-sized kitchen, the parish hall in the middle, and at the other end, a narrow foyer accessible from the outside or from the staircase, which led to the vestibule above. The foyer included two restrooms and my closeted sleeping space tucked under the stairs.

The youth group and a few young adults took on the tasks necessary to bring the coffee house to life. The Dodd brothers built a plywood platform that could comfortably hold three performers and then covered it with a large scrap of wall-to-wall carpeting they had left over from their job. Both boys worked for a carpet company, muscular arms and backs from laying carpet eight hours a day during the week flirted just below slightly snug flannel and denim. Next, they fashioned café tables from recycled industrial spools. The spools were once coiled with wire cable and transported to Alaska. The now empty spools were free for the taking, the electric company happy to get rid of them for lack of storage space. Lots of things were shipped to the state on spools or in crates or 55-gallon steel drums, and the discarded packaging cluttered the landscape—we were doing our part to recycle and put this material to good use.

As each table was finished, we covered the spool tops with red and white check tablecloths, vinyl coated for easy clean up. A few of us came up with a poster design which was transferred to a silk screen stencil so it could be inked, printed, and posted in libraries, bookstores, and coffee shops.

We worked late into Saturday night before we were to open the next evening, October 3, the youth group planning to sleep over right where we were to finish on time and clear out before Sunday services. Unrolling sleeping bags, they settled in for the night while I sat on a stool on our new built stage and read aloud to them a chapter from *Winnie the Pooh*, "In Which Christopher Robin Leads an Expotition to the North Pole." Before I was halfway through the chapter, the room had become still except for some light snoring, the bedtime story doing its magic. I closed the book, got off the stage, turned out the lights and went to my closet under the stairs.

The next morning, I woke early and went into the kitchen to start the coffee for congregants following services. The rattle of the tin measuring cup against the large coffee urn's basket provided an intentional reveille signaling to the troops that it was time to retreat to their homes before the early mass.

We opened that night. To be as inclusive as possible, I had permission to manage the coffee house as an outreach of the church but without the need to proselytize a blatant religious message. This pleased me. It was a place and time where you felt welcomed, regardless of what you believed. It was about community coming together through music experienced in ballads, work songs, spirituals, and protest songs. On any given Sunday evening you could hear covers of Phil Ochs, Peter, Paul and Mary, the Chad Mitchell Trio, Dylan, Baez, Ian and Sylvia, Leonard Cohen, Judy Collins, Tom Paxton, Gordon Lightfoot, and the Weavers—a mix of the familiar and new, songs from childhood and the Lower 48, about war and peace, home, love, and loss. For local singers and song writers, it was a welcome alternative to playing in the local

Anchorage bars where alcohol-fed behavior made it difficult to be heard or appreciated.

On these Sunday nights, the basement's singers and guests amplified warmth and well-being, shutting out the roaming wind circling around and around outside the door. The glow from hurricane lamps and votive candles pressed against our faces. Aromas of cinnamon, coffee and cookies added to the magic. We named the coffee house the *Poor Wind*.

Of all the performers who played at the Poor Wind, one connected with me, and has remained steadfast through all these many years, as a friend and confidant. A friendship that continues to this day and one that I cherish. Mary Wagner arrived in Anchorage two years before me by way of Seattle, a multitalented musician and teacher. We even performed together on occasion at the coffee house and during church services when we'd do a folk mass. We always seemed to be working on projects and planning future events, practicing duets, hanging posters around town, or just hanging out together sharing a good meal and conversation.

When I decided that my banjo alone wasn't always bringing the desired sound to certain pieces we were rehearsing, Mary directed me to L & J Music in downtown Anchorage, an extensive music store that sold all kinds of instruments from brass horns to reedy woodwind and string instruments of all kinds. It had a great guitar selection. We tried out several guitars, but when I discovered the Martin D12-20 hanging from a rack, I was sold. The sound was full and bright and could easily fill a room. As a musician, especially leading and accompanying large groups or a church congregation in song, it did what I needed it to do, without the need for other amplification. It also offered a distinct sound contrast to my banjo, which could get loud and edgy—I'd have to stuff a t-shirt or two between the head and dowel stick to muffle it—not always a perfect match to a quiet ballad or communion hymn.

I'd previously owned a Framus 12-string, but while running up the back stairs in my West Hall dorm at Westminster Choir College one Saturday afternoon, I tripped and fell on the guitar, smashing it to pieces. It looked like a dismembered marionette as I picked it up and swore. I'd take better care of this instrument, I vowed, mostly because it was the most expensive object I'd ever purchased.

After picking up the guitar, Mary and I drove back to the church, went into the sanctuary, and immediately ran through a few Ian and Sylvia songs, *Four Strong Winds, Song for Canada,* and *Early Morning Rain.* The instrument produced a heavenly sound further embellished by the church's excellent acoustics. My left-hand fingertips, though, would need to build up thick calluses to provide enough pressure to produce clear tones when pressing down the six pairs of strings.

Once we met, Mary became a constant in my life while in Alaska. Even though we were both slightly introverted, we were outgoing when we found ourselves performing in front of groups of people, regardless of the audience's size. Music was our catalyst for taking action and hopefully effecting positive change when working with others. The Poor Wind became our purpose and, more importantly, our passion.

To A Skyjacker Who Left This Morning

I

I saw you I think,
it was last night and alone
your gentle voice, and soft,
asked us, our friends,
on the value of proper ID
for the use of a borrowed
but not possessed half-fare card
and you were gentle but alone
and perhaps I caught some energy from you.

I don't know
what your business was
so late at the airport
and all you said was
that you'll have the bread by morning
and could leave.

And now I hear the plane
has gone to Cuba

and I know it was you,
don't ask me how
but maybe your questions
or maybe you and your gentle voice, and soft,
gave you away, but I know.

II
Seems like
things weren't going your way
seems like
you don't always get what you want
seems like
you'll never get up
and seems like
it's always over
but mostly it never really began.
Well, friend, I feel for you.

—October 18, 1971

I would often roam the concourse at Anchorage International Airport at night, sometimes alone, sometimes with friends. You didn't need a ticket or reason to be there. I went because it was a place that you could walk around in the dead of winter in your shirt sleeves without the bulky layers of cumbersome winter gear. I went because the airport held the promise for escape, the only way out, especially when looking out through the large plate glass windows at the handful of planes refueling and waiting at gates. There was something hopeful, reassuring, watching passengers board planes to somewhere else. I went because there was a decent restaurant that served the best Monte Cristo sandwiches I'd ever tasted.

One evening, after devouring my Monte Cristo, I was approached by a man maybe a little older than me. Pushing his horn-rimmed glasses back in place on the bridge of his nose, he asked our group about the need for a proper ID and something about an airline-issued half-fare card. I think the man might have been Dale Lavon Thomas, who on the next day, and at gunpoint, hijacked a Wien Consolidated Airlines 737 bound for Bethel. He demanded to be flown to Havana. A flight attendant on her first solo trip persuaded the hijacker to return to Anchorage to let off the passengers. The plane then headed for Vancouver before flying on to Mexico City with a flight plan ending in Havana. Dale, sometime mid-flight, had decided he wanted a larger, long-range jet and returned to Vancouver where he was arrested by a Royal Canadian Mounted Police inspector.

Chilkoot Charlies

ON THOSE WINTER NIGHTS WHEN I wasn't holding choir rehearsals, working as a relief counselor at one of Alaska Children's Services boys group homes, roaming the empty concourse at ANC, visiting friends, or hanging out with Mary or Mother Duffy at her Original Whole Earth Store, I'd usually be with Jim who ran errands and delivered prepared meals to the various group homes and shelters scattered across the city. Jim also played guitar and would help out at the Poor Wind whenever he could. When we had nothing better to do or just needed to get away from our day-to-day routines, we'd head out after his last delivery, radio blaring, driving way too fast on snow packed roads. On some nights, we'd drive through areas of ice fog as it prismed the rime topped streetlamps' sodium-vapor glare into shivering pillars of light suspended in ice crystals beaming forever upward. The old Chevy pickup's heater barely kept us warm, no match for the outside cold. Our combined laughter and giggles coated the windows with thin layers of cloudy frost, which required regular scraping on the inside of the windshield so we could see where we were going. The defroster was useless.

Our night adventures would sometimes include leaving the truck on the outskirts of Anchorage and hitching in one direction, it didn't matter where, and hoping, once we had tired of our adventuring, the next driver who came along and seeing our gloved thumbs signaling a need for a ride, would somehow return us to the vicinity of our abandoned vehicle. Jim relished in these excursions, embracing them as a break in the boredom of the long Alaskan winter. I saw it as a form of Russian roulette feeding my fear of being eaten by the next benevolent driver who would be way too willing to take us somewhere other than where we wanted to go; my mother's earlier warning of the link between cannibalism and hitchhiking playing out once again in my head.

The place I liked going to the most with Jim was Chilkoot Charlie's, a long narrow establishment in Spenard named after a fictional character dreamed up by local writer and radio host Ruben Gaines. The place was wild, a raw frontier spirit taking up space in a bar with outspoken owners, an outrageous staff, and an unchecked silliness. The atmosphere was only disrupted when someone would walk into the bar, revolver drawn and threatening to shoot the person who the night before was his best friend. Those disruptions didn't last long before the incident was forgotten, and the alcohol fueled revelry returned.

The long stretch of bar at the front entrance of Koot's, as it was affectionately called, didn't scare me a bit, even after the gun incident, but it was a threshold you had to cross to get to the larger room in the back where there were tables and music. A narrow pathway, it felt like passing through a gauntlet of beer guzzling mug-fisted men lined up against the wall and three deep along the bar, two towering walls of testosterone dwarfing all five-foot-six of me. The passage every time was a small price to pay for a chance to escape the confines of my basement closet and enjoy a local band or raucous piano player.

One of our favorite groups was the house band, The Rinky-Dinks. We also loved the cheap beer and mounds of peanuts, sometimes used as projectiles on unsuspecting first-time visitors or even the musicians themselves, heaped high in old prospector gold pans placed on each table. The band wore construction helmets for protection, as the unending supply of readily accessible ammo would be released for fun, and sometimes in anger, when alcohol leveraged sensibilities. The discarded husks covered the floor like spent shell casings. Everything about Koot's was good, except maybe for the service, which often seemed as if the wait staff had called out sick for the night or just hunkered down somewhere out of sight, especially when the peanuts started to fly.

When we had had enough, or more likely ran out of money, we jumped back into the pickup and headed out of Spenard, first to St. Mary's to drop me off before Jim completed the journey to his staff residence at the Jesse Lee Home for high-risk kids further out on Abbott Road.

One night on the way back from Koot's, we caught sight of a car that had slid off the highway at an unlit intersection and had ended up in a multilayered embankment of snow created by massive plows. If you paid attention, you could see how each previously plowed layer marked a specific snowfall, becoming part of a stratified collection of snow and ice, gravel and debris, and the remains of the occasional moose that had met its end in a collision. With each storm a slice of winter was left behind and added to the pile, where it would remain until the spring thaw released only that which would melt, leaving an aggregate of bones, skin, guts, and gravel behind.

We pulled over to offer assistance, a customary practice during winter months and a more frequent occurrence after the bars had closed and booze took over behind the wheel. Getting out of the pickup, we grabbed shovels from the back of the truck and proceeded to dig out the car and its occupants. We made sure everyone onboard was okay before we drove off, our night to be good Samaritans.

Back in the church's parking lot with the AM radio crackling a top 40's station we heard a new song for first time, Don McClean's

American Pie. We both loved it instantly. Taking advantage of the expanse of an empty lot and the whiskey and rye recklessness of the lyric, we drove in mad circles, skidding on ice and packed snow. We easily picked up the refrain, our voices hurtling through the pickup's cab and once again blinding the windshield in a thin film of ice, all the while singing about Chevys, levees, whiskey, and rye.

After a night a Koot's, I'd sometimes need to reconsider the draft board's use of the word *hardship* to describe the two years of alternative service I was ordered to complete as a conscientious object. I'd had an opportunity for an approved alternative service job at a coffee house managed by a social service agency in South Philly, and that only was possible because it was the required fifty-five miles from my home in Allentown; that distance from home met the stated hardship criteria that the Selective Service demanded. I wondered, because I had travelled so far from home if hardship was no longer the proper term in my situation. Sure, I was lonely, but that wasn't necessarily a hardship. I could be lonely anywhere. While I lived in a cramped closet, once the day ended and when no meetings or events were on the schedule for the night, I could enjoy unrestricted access to the entire church that I called home. The winter nights were endlessly long, but I had the Northern Lights to brighten the darkness. The summers felt like an extended celebration of daylight, nearly twenty hours a day around the solstice.

My hardship shifted from dealing with an inconvenient distance from home, just a nuisance really, had I accepted the Philly job, to something that really wasn't a hardship at all. Here I worked during the day and some evenings and went out at night and had a good time. It felt normal. I never had contact with my local draft board or the larger Selective Service agency during the entire time I was in Alaska. No one shouted orders at me or had me line up for roll call. No one checked if my waterbed was made. I could come and go as I pleased, but just couldn't leave.

Well, that's not completely true. I did have two brief earned vacations where I could fly home and back. The people at Alaska

Children's Services and Father Eddy recommended that getting out of the state every now and then was healthy, in some cases necessary when the emotional toll of working with kids in crisis would become overwhelming. The two brief times I did leave Alaska for a chance to see my parents back in Allentown, I'd spend my time aimlessly driving along country roads in my mother's car, going nowhere. I was always agitated and on edge whether I was in the house with my family or somewhere else; I just wanted to get back to Alaska and finish what I was sent there to do—complete my time as a conscientious objector. Maybe that was it, that not being able to leave of my own free will until my time was up, was what nagged at me and felt troublesome, a feeling just under the surface that gnawed at my independence.

Safekeeping

Anchorage, AK
May 3, 1972
Dear Herbie,

Went through my CO depression again. Also, I wept for what fools, white men are. The devastation and havoc our race have caused is something I can no longer face in any quiet or passive way. I have learned much from the Alaskan Natives here, from their ability to endure. I can hear it in their singing and see it when they dance. I have seen the destruction caused by alcohol and tuberculosis. Things we've introduced here.

Sunday I was in an adult Sunday school group. A woman who has a son being followed by the FBI for draft resistance, read a letter from a 23-year-old from Bangladesh.

The letter chronicled some of the atrocities committed during the Bangladesh Liberation War, including the genocidal rape of between 200,000 and 400,000 Bangladeshi women and girls. It was beyond disturbing. When she finished reading, I began to weep uncontrollably.

I could only cry. I couldn't stop crying. I finally had to leave the room. Mary Eddy, the priest's wife, came after me and we walked for a while. It felt like things had been building inside me over the last few weeks regarding the war and being a CO.

I know that it is important for me to follow through on my commitments. I am a CO for 24 months, but damn it, there is only so much one can take and then you break, and you say you will not follow that anymore. I no longer carry my draft card; I gave it to Mary for now.

The draft is unjust. Its energy is totally negative, authoritative, and bureaucratic with a holier than thou attitude. Why must we judge each other? Why are we so inhuman? I need to work out these feelings I'm struggling with into music or an art piece rather than becoming too radical. I'll try to remain passive.

You told me many times, years ago, that anarchy is the only true form of government. I did not always follow what you meant but respected your thoughts on this. I think I understand it better now. I have seen it work beautifully here in Alaska, especially in more remote areas, especially among certain homesteaders.

I've been told that I should go easier on mankind, that we are all basically good. I still cannot see that. Maybe my anger is blocking my ability to understand that right now. I'm trying to be part of the universe in a way that is positive and peaceful, rather than being part of the violence or causing pain.

I am glad I have you for a friend. I am glad I can write you and get this shit off my chest. I would enjoy talking with you in person right now.

Love,
Buzzy

p.s. . . . I'm sending you my journal as I'm feeling a bit destruc-
tive at the moment. I guess it's similar to me giving Mary my
draft card. Take care of it for me.

Herb, and later together with his wife, Linda, held onto that journal for decades, hidden for safekeeping in Linda's top bureau draw where she kept her favorite scarves. Herb had also held onto every letter I mailed him, more than seventy-five of them, during my time in Alaska. They sent the journal back to me when I asked for it a few years ago. Herb also made copies of a few letters from the beginning of my journey to Alaska and sent those along as well. He has now returned all the original letters to me, in their postmarked envelopes. He said some were so disturbing that they were still hard to read. Disturbing or not, the letters he kept safe for me have now become a kind of memory quilt, like the ones made from the sewn together pieces of clothing of loved ones who've passed on; the kind that when you fall asleep under one, you begin to dream the dreams of the ancestors that continue to live in the pieced together covering. The difference here is that I'm not sleeping under a stack of letters, but reading them, recreating the once lived pattern of my life into a satisfying design that brings meaning and makes sense.

Unfortunately, by the time I sent the journal to Herb for safe-keeping, I had already destroyed all the letters he sent me during my time in Alaska, as well as most poems and stories I had writ-ten and music I had composed. The evidence of my defeatist men-tal state, especially when things didn't go my way, could be seen in the occasional small ash mounds in the church parking lot—the scattered remains of personal sacrificial bonfires. Now, with these letters in hand, I can see that each period of depression and destruction followed a timeline which corresponded to a specific postmarked envelope and described in detail in the contents of the enclosed letter I'd sent to Herb.

Today when I read the journal or any of my letters to Herb, I pic-ture myself back then as a naive young man, way too self-centered and lacking confidence. I tried to make sense out of the world by forcing it to adhere to my needs and wants, rather than learning how to be more accepting of the impact my environment, all aspects of it from the emotional and social to the physical, had on me. Some journal entrees and letters make no sense at all. Grammar had deteriorated to nothing more than run on sentences for pages, rambling words and rants that now seem troubling or in some cases, embarrassingly immature and silly, obvious evidence that I was completely lost, lonely and needing more help than I was getting, or allowing myself to receive.

I've reread the letters I wrote to Herb over those two years in Alaska. The majority sent to him in the first few months after I arrived. Always stating how much I missed him, loved him, asking when he'd come for a visit, which he never did, or sometimes asking him to move here all together. The letters went out daily in the beginning, but no fewer than two a week. I can only imagine what the person slotting mail for faculty and staff at the Hackley School where Herb worked thought about the scores of letters arriving for him from Alaska. Herb had the music teaching job that was supposed to be mine had I not been drafted. I was able to put in a good word about him to the headmaster and he offered Herb the position. I never considered how my constantly writing him might look, how he felt about it or if it generated any gossip in the faculty dining hall.

I thought, maybe Mary Lee Nicholson was on to something right before I lost my job at the Anchorage Children's Christian Home when she told me, "I think you're suffering, a little bit crazy right now."

The *little bit crazy* seemed situational, however, as there were moments of clarity and purpose, stability, and satisfaction, especially when I was working with music; and then at other times, like hearing the story of the young Bangladeshi or impulsively destroying Herb's letters, I'd experience a total meltdown and feelings of hopelessness.

Shelter

THE CHURCH'S EDUCATION BUILDING WASN'T USED during the summer months. The Sunday school and religious education classes along with the Monday through Friday morning pre-school that kept the building active from September through May, were on hiatus. While the church might not draw its regular crowd of worshippers and toddlers in these warmer months, the Alaskan summers, however, did call to people, mostly from the Lower 48, seeking adventure, recreation, and escape. Once these travelers found themselves in this last frontier, the realization soon hit that everything cost at least double to what food, lodging, gas, and other daily necessities did back home. Some soon found themselves broke and in need of a place to stay and food to eat.

A few hopefuls, failing to do their research, arrived looking for work thinking that construction of the planned Trans-Alaska pipeline from Prudhoe Bay to Valdez was already in full gear, especially considering that the vast Prudhoe Bay oil field had been discovered a few years earlier, in 1968, but the oil sat untapped. While piles of pipe waited to be laid, environmental, legal, and political haggling held up construction for years. It wasn't until the gasoline shortage in 1973, which caused long lines at the pump and led to the implementation of even-odd days fuel rationing at filling stations across the country, that lawmakers finally acted and passed legislation that would officially launch construction of the pipeline in 1975. But those that thought they'd get rich fast laying pipe during the summers of 1971 and 1972 would have to wait.

Others came to Alaska to escape, the state offering the distance away from the Lower 48 they needed to hide out for a while or maybe forever; to let whatever they had done or had forced them to flee to die down before risking a return home.

Seeing the need and having ample unused space from late June to the end of August, Father Eddy decided to offer up the education building as a temporary shelter for those in need. With my music responsibilities for Sunday services and working with the youth group not in demand during the summer, Chuck wanted me to manage the shelter. I would connect the temporary residents with social service agencies if needed, familiarize them with local grocery stores and pharmacies, and do whatever it took, within reason, to help them get back on their feet so that they could return home before fall arrived. We held the belief that, because we were a church, the shelter would be a refuge to those who ended up here regardless of their background, as long as our small community was safe, we didn't ask a lot of questions—unless it became necessary to do so.

Empty classrooms made great temporary living quarters. There were enough cots on hand and families could share one room. Singles got a room to themselves unless we were too crowded. If that happened, we could set up rooms as separate dorms for men and women. Residents had open access to a pantry stocked with donated canned and dry goods—peas, corn, green and baked beans, flour, sugar, lentils, rice, and other grains. The church's kitchen was also available for food preparation.

We limited stays to no more than a week in most cases, and that might have been a regulation stipulated by the city or state, not quite sure. Maybe it was a way to keep residents from getting too comfortable with the offer of free housing or treating their stay like a paid all-inclusive Alaskan vacation. If people still needed help after their allotted time, I'd contact social services for their assistance in securing another shelter or safe place for them to go.

The people we served were grateful to be with us for a few days or longer. We also asked that weapons not be brought into the building, for everyone's safety. No one ever gave me a problem with that request, well almost never, and other problems were quickly resolved like finding an extra cot or helping someone light a burner on the church's commercial stove or helping a family learn how to navigate a large grocery store. That last one had me chuckling to myself once the ordeal was over and I was alone.

* * *

An Alaska Native family from the interior was staying with us while more permanent housing could be finalized in Anchorage. The family had never ventured far from their village and arriving in Anchorage would have been a somewhat overwhelming experience for them. As the Bureau of Indian affairs readied the family's new home, a social worker asked me to take the family shopping for groceries before they officially moved in later that day. I took the family to a Carrs, a large grocery store like those in the Lower 48. Prior to departing for the store, I sat down with the parents and helped them generate a groceries list. I assumed, which I shouldn't have, that we'd list items by categories, making it easier to navigate the store. After the first list was made, the teacher in me explained how we could rearrange items by dairy, meats, cereals, soft goods, cleaning supplies and so on. I also mentioned how the store was arranged in sections, I even drew a diagram, so hunting for the items they needed would be made easier for them. They smiled and nodded as if they understood me. Once at the store it didn't seem to go as planned—*the best laid schemes o' Mice an' Men . . .*

We got through the first two items on the list in sequence, as I had planned, but then, whether it was the florescent lights overhead, the overabundance and variety of products, colors, sale signs, announcements from above, "cleanup on aisle six," it all went to hell. The list was lost and forgotten along with the detailed diagram of the store. The couple moved from dairy to cleaning supplies, back to dairy for butter, back to cleaning supplies for dish detergent. It was mad random chaos. I surrendered, waiting near the bank of checkout lanes, catching glimpses of the couple as they cut down aisles and across rows, bouncing in step to the upbeat music piped in to keep shoppers happy and spending their hard-earned dough on things they most likely didn't need, tossing items in their cart, smiling, and having the time of their lives. It was like watching a chase scene in some old slapstick movie, the Stooges or Abbot and Costello, in a corridor of slamming doors, the good guys pursued by ghosts, cops, robbers, monsters and the like. When it was over, the couple had somehow miraculously gathered everything they needed, were thrilled, and energized by the experience. I was exhausted.

* * *

THERE WAS ONE INCIDENT, HOWEVER, THAT could have turned deadly. A family of three, the Smiths, arrived sometime in mid-July, all blond, blue eyed and tan—mother Sarah, stepfather John and twelve-year-old Billy. Their story was vague in how they ended up here in Anchorage, but somewhere in their telling of it mentioned about leaving California and wanting to see some of Alaska's many wonders. Sarah always seemed nervous, skittish, as if waiting for something to go wrong, whether it was in preparing a meal for her family or venturing off to the local laundromat. The boy, Billy, was quiet and only spoke to me or Father Eddy when his stepdad was around and within earshot, careful with his words, watching for John's approval before he said anything to us. Billy did take me for a ride on his Honda SL70, a minibike that was introduced in the late 1960s that resembled a street motorcycle more than the trail bike that it was. They came ready for an Alaskan adventure.

The family's stay at the shelter did not go smoothly. On one Sunday night alone, I ended up at the hospital two times when John got himself into a couple downtown barroom brawls. Leaving his wife and stepson here at the church, at least, kept them safe. I didn't get back to my closet until 3:00 a.m.

During the ordeal, when John wasn't within earshot, Sarah quietly let me know that maybe Billy would be better off with his natural father in California and asked if I'd help contact him. I'd begin working on that after I'd gotten some much needed sleep. The reality was, once I tried to locate Billy's dad, that it was easier said than done. I kept at it during the week and even connected with social workers I had worked with while at Alaska Children's Services, but each lead I got turned out to be a dead end.

The next Saturday, which would be the family's last day at the shelter, John came back to the church with a ton of groceries, mostly meats. His haul seemed so much more than the two-week supply of food I'd shopped for when working at the teenage boys group home. John asked to use the large refrigerator in the church's kitchen to store some of the perishable items, which turned out to be steaks, chops, roasts, chicken, enough for a village feast, all very expensive because these products had to be flown into Alaska from the Lower 48. I asked him why so much food. He mentioned he had made some friends in the area and had picked up food for a neighborhood cookout that afternoon. He said they all chipped in. He had purchased the food at a different branch of Carrs, not the one near the church, but one closer to where the party would take place, he told me. He'd take the food from the fridge when he went over later.

So maybe I was a tad bit naive, but I didn't think too much more about it until John came over to the church around two o'clock looking for me. He said the neighborhood gathering had been cancelled, something about someone not feeling well or some other family crisis that caused it to be cancelled at the last minute. He needed to take the food back to the store so he could get a refund and return the money to his new friends. He wanted me to drive him to the branch of the market near the church, no need for me to take him to the one farther away. He said that he would've done it himself, but Sarah had taken their truck to do the laundry. I agreed to drive him, and we loaded up my VW for the short drive to the market. He asked me to wait in the car, that this would only take a minute. Grabbing a stray shopping cart left in the parking lot, he loaded the bags of food and went into the store.

It's hard to believe the market would consider taking back all that meat, but it did. It's expensive and was just purchased a few hours ago, he had the receipt after all, even with it being from a different branch of the grocery chain, this store should be able to process his return. But something felt off as John moved quickly from the store and back to my car.

"Okay, let's go!" John had a wad of cash that he was stuffing into his front jean's pocket.

"Do you want me to drive you to your friends so you can return their money?"

"No, I can do that later when Sarah's back from the laundromat. Just take me to the church."

We arrived back at the church, John going to his room in the education building. I went up to the choir loft to go over the hymns for Sunday's service.

In the late afternoon I took a walk through the education building, checking in with the guests, seeing if they needed anything, and to learn of any next steps in either their returning home or finding a more permanent place to stay. We only had the Smiths, a young man from Lebanon, Wael, and a church family's nineteen-year-old son, Chris Chalifour, staying with us at the time. My walk-through would be quick.

I didn't see the latter two men around; I didn't think they were in the building. As I approached the far set of doors leading to the parking lot, I heard noise coming from the last room on my left, the room where the Smiths were staying. I had almost reached the exit door when I turned around to find Sarah and Billy standing in front of John, each of them clutching their backpacks and sleeping bags. John gripped a pistol which was aimed directly at me. The pistol looked like the one my dad owned; it could do some damage. I froze, but somehow didn't panic. In fact, I was thinking clearly enough to ask a question.

"John, what's going on? We don't allow weapons in the building."

"Don't move. We're leaving."

Just then I realized I'd have to move if they were going to get out of the building. I was blocking their escape with me standing between them, the door, and their freedom. In the narrow hallway there was no place for me to step aside, no room I could jump into, no trap door in the floor to drop me out of this mess. We'd have to agree on a maneuver, like a sequence of dance moves to work our way around each other, a tango, no, it had to be something like *La Danse Apache*. Two things were going through my mind. One, I was disappointed, because I saw myself as a nice guy trying to do nice things for people in need and this was hurting me. Two, I was trapped, backed into a dead-end alley, and now beginning to really fear for my life.

John hadn't said any more. I don't know if he had anything else to say or whether he couldn't think of anything else to say. Sarah and Billy were beginning to lose it. I heard Sarah whisper a plea to John, to make this stop, to agree to leave peacefully. I wanted him to just put his gun down. I had no idea why he was acting like this or why his behavior had changed since earlier that day.

Just then I noticed a change in the pattern of light coming in through the door window behind me. It was a shadow. I heard the door open. The shadow was replaced by Father Eddy, who towered over both me and John. He moved beside me, then took up guard in front of me, facing John and the gun. John remained shielded by Sarah and Billy.

Chuck broke the stalemate's silence. Where a minute before John and I had nothing to say, Chuck now spoke in calming terms, making sense, and somehow reaching John's blocked mind. John lowered the gun. Chuck offered to take it, to put it in the church safe for now. John declined the offer, placing the gun in the back of his jean's waistband. We moved so that Chuck and I were on one side of the hallway, giving space for the Smiths to leave. Chuck's final words of parting, "It's probably best that you don't come back. If you truly care about your family, then straighten out your life. If you're running, find a way to stop. If you're in trouble, make amends."

When Chuck and I got to the parking lot we watched as the pickup sped off spitting gravel into the air with the trail bike ricocheting against the walls of the truck. Working together, we each attempted to memorize one half of the California license plate to be sure we got it. Chuck and I made it to the church office to call the police. We reported what had happened, giving descriptions of John, Sarah and Billy, their pickup truck and license plate number to the officer on the phone. We also told him that John was armed. We later learned that John Smith, if that was his real name, had run a scam at the grocery store, buying meats and supplies at one branch of the market using ill-gotten food stamps and forged checks and then returning them to a different location for cash. There were also warrants out for his arrest back in California, facing charges I no longer can remember.

Once the encounter was over and the police report made, Chuck invited me back to the rectory to debrief. He made us each one of his bourbon and lemonades, clearly for medicinal purposes this time around. He asked me how I was doing, told me I could talk about what had happened with him anytime. For some reason my often-buried New England stoicism chose to surface at that moment and told him I was fine; but as Chuck's wife, Mary, often noticed about me, I could be read like an open book, I wore my heart on my sleeve, and carried a gay chip on my shoulder, regardless of what I was trying to hide. The gay chip was more subtle, but Mary saw it, a frustration and sometimes concealed anger that I could be ostracized for just being who I was.

Breakdown II

I COULDN'T SHAKE IT. I HAD JUST WOKEN UP from an afternoon nap in my closet. I was awake but had what seemed like two completely different realities playing out in front of me. One was me in the basement of the church, plenty of summer light flooding through the windows, everything in focus. In the other, I was floating in the sky in some sort of numinous reality, which didn't seem possible, but that's what was happening. I made my way to the door leading outside.

Just then, my Lebanese friend, Wael, who was staying next door in the shelter, opened the door and came into the parish hall. He joked with me about how he didn't feel well. Something he frequently say to start up a conversation, to provoke a "tell-me-what's-wrong" response from anyone nearby. He was always fine, and charming.

I, on the other hand, was not at all fine. I could clearly make out Wael, all the details in what he was saying along with the physical space where we were standing. My other reality was simultaneously taking place and it had nothing to do with where he and I stood facing each other. I was experiencing a complete lack of identity, a feeling of being hollow, soulless, as if I didn't exist. Competing with Wael and his surroundings was a growing awareness, more like a vision of deep space, stars, and galaxies with me somehow speeding through them. I was aware of a ladder floating sideways right beside me with heads of old men hovering between the rungs. Faces I interpreted as Beethoven, DaVinci and Christ, among others, images seemingly taken out of H. W. Janson's *History of Art:* a combination of oil portraits and marble busts hovering in space.

"Wael, buddy, I'm not well either. I need to leave." He looked at me and knew something was wrong and walked beside me, guiding me toward the rectory.

He rapped on the door. Mary Eddy, Chuck's wife answered almost immediately.

"Mrs. Eddy, I think something is wrong with Don."

I went in the house as Wael handed me off to Mary and made his way back to the education building that doubled as a shelter for stranded travelers and others during the summer months.

I found a place on the couch in the living room next to the fireplace and sat down.

Mary had been talking with a friend, Karol Libby. The Buddha (Charles, Jr.), Chuck and Mary's baby boy was playing on the floor. I asked Mary to maybe have Karol take Buddha to another room for the moment, for his safety really.

Karol picked up Buddha and headed to his bedroom.

The sense of speeding through space seemed to intensify. I was being pulled farther and farther away from reality, in a state of awe, attracted to it as I was being drawn deeper into the experience and wanting to resist it, to escape it at the same time—*mysterium tremendum et fascinans.* There was something important for me to discover about the ladder that was still hovering beside me. I thought maybe if I could get on the other side of it, I'd discover what was happening to me, what this all meant, to uncover a secret, an understanding about life. The famous floating heads remained in view. I wanted this feeling to end, needed it to all stop, but I didn't know how. Then I saw the set of fireplace tools by the hearth. The poker seemed liked the answer. If I could get to the poker, grip it with enough force, I could bash it against the side of my head and maybe knock this demon out of me, or at least knock myself out.

Mary sat beside me on the couch. She held on to me, a continuous hug as I struggled to find control. She had me talk out what I was feeling, what I was seeing. I told her I had been sleeping, just taking a nap. When I woke up it felt like I wasn't there anymore.

She held on, encouraging me to breathe in a steady and controlled manner, to focus on my breath. A few more minutes passed and then it stopped. Just plain old stopped as if nothing had been going on in my head. The visions were gone, I felt whole again, although drained. Mary got me a glass of water. I thanked her profusely, and Karol too, while tears continued to stream down my face.

Mary kept me at the rectory for another half hour just to be sure I was over it. We had tea with honey. I then made my way back to the church and sought out Wael in the shelter to thank him.

Later in the afternoon, Chuck stopped by to see how I was doing. We found a quiet place to talk. Mary had told him what had happened. I confirmed her story and added a few other details. He asked a couple more questions.

"What was happening right before you felt this way?"

"I was napping, maybe for a half hour, nothing else."

"Did you go out last night, have anything to drink?"

"Nope, I was here working on music."

"Did you take anything? Drugs, LSD? From what Mary said it sounds like you were hallucinating."

"No, nothing."

"Okay, if you experience anything else like that again call or come get me right away."

I told Chuck I would, however, after the experience ended, I felt somehow renewed, more aware of my surroundings, the people

I was around, and a sense of control, even though I had just lost complete control a couple hours before. Looking back now, I most likely was suffering from a form of situational depression, a temporary state triggered by stress or a traumatic event, or a series of events. Within months I had lost my job at Anchorage Children's Christian Home, had to give up my apartment in exchange for living in a storage closet under the stairs of a church, and had a gun drawn on me. Added to all of this was the fact that while I was out prior to coming to Alaska, I now seemed to struggle with my identity, keeping that part of my life secret from others, except for Chuck and Mary Eddy. I also struggled with being a conscientious objector. Somehow, I thought once I received my CO status, that I would be protected, left unscathed by violence or situations like having someone wield a weapon against me. Clearly CO status didn't come with a superhero's emblem emblazoned on a cape that announced my pacifistic stand. There was nothing for me to physically display so that others could see this part of my life. I realized then that my pacifism would only be evident to others through my deeds, my day-to-day interactions with those I'd encounter. Just being a conscientious objector, a declared pacifist, didn't shield me from forces outside my control or from those who saw my stand as weakness.

That one depressive episode was the only time it happened. Even a month later while visiting a family I knew from the church who was spending some time camping near Bird Creek twenty miles south of Anchorage, a friend of theirs had pulled a large Bowie knife on me after learning that I was a CO. He called me un-American as I opted to make my way to my car and head back to Anchorage. This incident didn't seem to affect me or provoke a repeat of what I'd experienced that Saturday afternoon just a few weeks earlier.

Chuck and I continued our weekly chats, therapy sessions really, but we didn't call them that. Mary on the other hand had me regularly meet with her at the dining room table where she'd have me sample Rorschach tests or complete mental health surveys as part of a psychology course she was taking at the University of Alaska. I didn't think too much of it at the time, but as these sessions went on it dawned on me that Mary may have been trying to help me or at least open me up to some clues as to my mental stability. Either way, I did enjoy interpreting those ink blots.

Build You a Mind

M ARY WAGNER, MY FOLK SINGING FRIEND, also did her part to be supportive when I would turn fragile, but with a snap-out-of-it delivery. No holding back, but always compassionate in her desire to lift me up.

Usually, in addition to singing together and working to make the Poor Wind coffee house a welcoming venue for musicians and the people who'd come to hear them perform, Mary and I would just find time to hang out together as good friends do. Some nights we would make the drive down Turnagain Arm toward Girdwood for the Double Muskie Inn, at the time a rustic roadhouse off an old mail route at the edge of an Alaskan rainforest. Turning off the highway and riding down that often-rutted trail was a magical experience, especially after a fresh snow had weighed down huge Alpine spruce branches, not the scrawny black spruce that were common around the city, causing a green and white canopy all the way to the inn. The Double Muskie was a great place to kick back, enjoy a beer or two, a decent meal and listen to local musicians, mostly folk music, some who had played at the Poor Wind. Back then you could grill your own meal, usually a steak or sometimes reindeer hotdogs, over open flames in the dining room's fireplace. I never did that, but usually opted for the pizza, wood fire-grilled and loaded with vegetables.

One night in April or May, months before my astral projection meltdown, instead of venturing down the highway to the double Muskie, Mary and I went to the Fourth Avenue Theater to see *Far from the Madding Crowd*, the 1967 adaptation of the Thomas Hardy classic featuring Julie Christie, Terrence Stamp, Peter Finch, and Alan Bates. It seemed like current films, television shows and pop music took forever, in this case four years, to make their way north to Alaska.

We were in the seasonal phase in Alaska referred to as *breakup*, that long stretch of overcast days that marks the fluctuating weather between the dark of winter and light of summer. Using *spring* as the word to describe this in-between time doesn't accurately capture this state of limbo, of melting ice and snow, greasy roads and potholes, and mud that often freezes solid during the night only to thaw again during the increasing hours of daylight. River ice across the state breaks up causing ice jams and flooding, the whole thing a meteorological mess.

With breakup in full force, I couldn't only blame Hardy's Victorian tale and the movie's stunning yet bleak setting in the rural landscapes of southwest England for the reaction I had after viewing the film, but it was certainly a contributing factor. One scene sent me over the edge. The scene that replayed in my mind and kept me up at night, was when the younger and more impulsive of two sheep dogs mischievously releases a herd of penned sheep late at night, driving them over an enormous seaside cliff, all 200 animals, including pregnant ewes and those waiting still to be born, meeting their untimely gruesome deaths on the desolate beach below: the herder, Gabriel, then ending the scene by shooting his wayward dog dead. I couldn't get past that early moment in the film; the rest of it, the remaining two plus hours was a blur to me, causing me to lose most of the film's details along with its storyline.

We left the theater with Mary behind the wheel. As she drove, I began to weep uncontrollably. Reaching over and touching my arm she asked what was wrong and I did my best, between sobs, to relay to her what I was feeling—some element of existential dread, a feeling of lacking any groundedness or sense of purpose.

Mary pulled the car over, let it idle, and looked at me.

"Donald, we need to build you a mind. Help you get some discipline up here," she said as she pointed to, then tapped the side of my head.

Mary didn't have specific steps for me to follow in building my mind and she never mentioned it again. It was in her actions, taking time for us to sing together, to provide a routine with expectations and tasks, like preparing a set for us to perform at the Poor Wind or our late-night journeys to the Double Muskie or trips to the Mahoney brothers' compound near Wasilla—three adjoining 180-acre homesteads with what appeared to be a small village the brothers had built where the individual parcels of land intersected. Mary's ultimate winning strategy was being my friend, lifelong to this very day.

RANT

DECEMBER 8, 1971

IT WAS GOOD TO TALK WITH YOU TONIGHT. VERY GOOD IN FACT.

I AM GLAD WE CAN TALK. AND THINGS ARE FINE.

SOMETIMES WORDS ARE HARD TO USE. I'M HAVING THAT PROBLEM RIGHT NOW. THERE SEEMS TO BE A TIME WHERE SOME OF THE BEAUTY OF THIS WORLD CAN EXIST. AND MAYBE WITH THAT TIME, A PLACE. AND TOGETHER THESE TIMES AND PLACES THAT WE HAVE NOW WILL BECOME THAT TIME AND PLACE WHERE YOU AND I WILL LIVE. IT IS HARD TO HAVE A MOTHER I WOULD IMAGINE LIKE YOURS. IT IS SO DIFFICULT TO BE, REALLY ON YOUR OWN AND TO BREAK TIES OR RATHER SENSITIVELY UNDERSTANDING THOSE TIES. MEANWHILE THE WORLD BECOMES ONE BIG FUCK UP BUT I NOW SMILE AT THE WHOLE (HOLE, ASS) FUCKING, DAMN PLACE. BECAUSE

THE WHOLE (ASS HOLE) FUCKING, DAMN PLACE IS
REALLY PART OF IT (SHIT) (RATHER SHIT FROM THE
ASS, WHOLE, HOLE) AND IF THE FOOLS AND NOT
SO FOOLS FEEL LIKE FUCKING IT ALL UP, WELL IT'S
ALL RIGHT BY ME, AS LONG AS THEY DON'T FUCK
ME UP WITH IT, BECAUSE, YOU SEE, OR DON'T YOU
SEE, THAT WHO HAS GIVEN THESE PEOPLE THE
RIGHT TO CREATE MATERIALISM AND ABOVE ALL
THE RIGHT TO ETC. ETC. ETC. IS NONE OTHER
THAN NOBODY. FUCK. MEANWHILE YOU ARE
NOT FUCKED UP AND I'M PRETTY SURE I'M NOT
FUCKED UP SO WE ARE STUCK WITH TWO THINGS:
a, THE BLAME (WHICH IS NOT OURS) AND b, THE
POWER TO DO ABSOLUTELY NOTHING ABOUT IT.
SO WHY BOTHER. BUT I HAVE TO BOTHER ABOUT
SOMETHING, SO I BOTHER ABOUT YOU. I CARE
ABOUT YOU AND LOVE YOU. SO I GO HOME SOON
TO SEE THE FOLKS AND THAT'S ALL I CARE ABOUT,
EXCEPT I WANT TO SEE YOU, AND SOMETIMES I
DON'T THINK YOU CARE IF WE EVER SEE EACH
OTHER AGAIN AND I SEE THAT THIS IS NOT
THE CASE FOR I AM EQUIPPED WITH A SPECIAL
MALFUNCTIONING ANTI-TRUST SENSITIVITY
WARNING DEVICE THAT HAS NEVER ONCE
WORKED PROPERLY BUT AM NOW AWARE WHEN
IT DOES WORK NOT TO LISTEN TO IT ANYMORE,
BUT THAT IS OF ANOTHER TIME. I AM PRETTY
ACCURATE (BRAG) OF FEELINGS AND MAYBE
BEETHOVEN IS AROUND AND MAYBE YOU'RE
JESUS CHRIST, BUT I DOUBT THAT, YOU'RE HERBIE
CHRIST, BUT NOT YET AND I'M NOT ANYTHING
RIGHT NOW. SO MAYBE WHEN THE LEAD WEIGHT
FINALLY PULLS YOU DOWN SO FAR THAT YOU
CAN'T GET UP WITHOUT HELP AND WHEN YOU

GET REALLY FUCKED UP WITH EVERYTHING ELSE, YOU'LL COME HERE, NOT THAT ALASKA IS THE ANSWER, BUT THE ANSWER WILL PROBABLY BE US TOGETHER, AND THAT WILL BE A GOOD TIME AND WHEREVER A GOOD PLACE. WHEN YOU FRIEND ANSWERED THE PHONE, "BUZZY?" I THOUGHT IT WAS YOUR FATHER. SO, WHAT CAN I SAY …

…I HAVE GROWN SO VERY FOND OF MOUNTAINS THAT THEY NOW EQUAL MY LOVE FOR THE SEA. WHICH I NEVER THOUGHT I WOULD FIND MYSELF THINKING, SAYING OR WRITING. THE FIRST TIME I WAS DEEP REALLY DEEP IN THE MOUNTAINS WAS IN BRITISH COLUMBIA AND THE YUKON ON MY JOURNEY HERE. I WAS SCARED A BIT AND COULD ONLY THINK THAT THOSE VERY TALL PILES OF ROCK COULD NOT BE TOO STURDY AND MIGHT FALL DOWN ON TOP OF ME. NOW I SEE THAT THEY ARE EXTREMELY WELL STRUCTURED AND "FIRM" AND I WOULD NEVER THINK OF MOVING ONE AS A JOKE. SO, WHERE ARE WE?

WOW TIME FOR SLEEP AND DREAMS ONE OF MY MOST EXCITING AVOCATIONS. I BELIEVE IN YOU AS A BASICALLY GOOD PERSON WITH AN EARNEST AND SENSITIVE MIND. I USE "BASICALLY" BECAUSE "GENERALLY" ISN'T AS GOOD FOR THE CHARACTER. FUCK. I'M SORRY. GOODNIGHT THANKS FOR READING THIS. I DON'T TYPE LETTERS VERY MUCH. PEACE.

Mind Control

I T WAS LATE AFTERNOON, ALREADY DARK, so it must have been winter still, when we arrived at either a professional office building with a classroom or maybe a conference room. Or was it somewhere on the campus of Anchorage Community College? I can't remember. I do remember the ground floor entrance at the end of the building, a small table for registration, a hallway leading off to the left and beyond that, a staircase leading up to the floors above. Sitting at the small table working a checklist and handing out name tags was an older woman, dyed blond hair perfectly coifed, with fortune teller eyes and large hands.

The poster behind the table read *Silva Mind Control* and kitty-cornered on the top right was a glossy 8x10 of Jose Silva, a former electronics repairman turned parapsychologist. On the other corner of the poster, another 8x10 of our facilitator, Gloria Whitehead. In her photo, Gloria resembled a character actor from a fifties sit-com, hair teased out a bit more than how she now wore it sitting in front of us at the table; but with the same overdone make up as if she was ready for her next closeup. She still wore the same large-lensed glasses, each lens cut in an unfinished oval, arcing at the top but not quite finishing its curve at the bottom where they seemed to cut into her large cheeks. She reminded me of the cartoon character, Petunia Pig.

The outcomes listed on the poster for this three-day workshop suggested that through positive visualization, hypnotic suggestion, and perception in altered states, you could heal both yourself and others, enhance memory and learning, and increase one's telepathic powers.

The workshop included a fee but was waived for medical professionals and clergy. I was neither and lacked the kind of funds that would allow me to pay the price for admission. When it was my turn at the table to enroll and beg for a deferred payment plan, our facilitator, Gloria, seemed to pause. She placed a hand on my forearm and studied my face. She asked why I had decided to join her workshop. I said it interested me. She asked what I did. I told her I was a conscientious objector fulfilling my two years of alternate service at St. Mary's and with Alaska Children's Services.

"Oh, how wonderful, your fee is waived." Amazing, I thought and just like that I was enrolled. She then asked the unexpected question of the evening, loud enough that the others around us could hear.

"Tell me now, Don," already on a first name basis, "have you ever seen or encountered a UFO, a flying saucer?"

I thought I'd better sit down in the chair next to her at the sign-in table. She still had a determined hold on my arm.

I had seen a flying saucer once or some form of unexplainable apparition, maybe a few times, including the glowing orbs I had witness as a teenager and more recently at St. Mary's, until I was in my late twenties when the visions seemed to stop. This one time I think it came from outer space. We lived in rural north central Massachusetts in the house my father built, I was eight. Something shiny caught my eye in the early evening summer sky. I went to a living room corner window and looked out and just at treetop level of a stand of white pines there it was—a metallic disc floating, just hovering in one spot over the tree-framed clearing.

"Daddy, look!" But by the time my father joined me at the window, the object was gone.

I went to bed, falling asleep under the midnight blue canopy of pasted gold stars of my built-in knotty pine alcove bed. The next morning, I woke to the sound of a robin outside my window, its call instantly triggering a sharp pain in my head. When I went downstairs to the kitchen, my mother handed me a drawing of a circular object with a slight tail.

"I drew this after Daddy and I saw this by your bedroom window last night and wondered if this is what you saw outside the living room window." It wouldn't be the only time my parents witnessed an apparition dogging me.

I took the drawing and saw the familiar shape of what I had seen the night before. I smiled.

"Yes, that's what I saw. It was all shiny and moved away fast."

Now, as an adult, I know that I can rely on my life experiences, prior knowledge, and the current technology to make sense out of things I don't quite understand, to look for patterns, repetition, and clues to bring form to the new and unfamiliar. What I knew when I was eight about objects in the sky was limited to birds in flight, the stars and moon at night, the occasional plane that flew over our house, and Flash Gordon's rocket. I loved Flash Gordon, the serial that aired in the mid-fifties.

Sitting on the floor in front of the television set, I felt a certain crush-like thrill whenever Buster Crabbe would appear. Of all the episodes, one remains etched in the black and white spaceograph embedded in my mind: "Battling the Sea Beast." Flash was all man standing there in his almost knee-high space boots, squared-off tight black shorts, big belt, shirtless and trapped in the water tank and forced to fight the dreaded Octosak. Rubbery tentacles extending, reaching full length to coil around my hero's torso, legs, and arms, twisting around Flash's neck.

Maybe the manifestation of what I saw through the living room window that night was made flesh because of that old black and white series; the rocket ship becoming the reference for bringing meaning to something unexplainable. It didn't explain how my parents also saw something nearly identical hours later on the other side of the house after I went to sleep.

I told Gloria I believed I had seen a UFO as a child and she wrote down four letters, all capitalized and slid it across the surface to me, like two spies passing secret coded messages to each other. "Do these letters look familiar or mean something to you?"

I looked at the letters. OXHO or perhaps a different sequence of the same letters, it's been a long time since I've thought about this. She also suggested I read a book. Something with *Aquarian* or *Aquarianists* in the title and told me there were hundreds if not thousands of people who had been contacted by the aliens. These people, she said, would become the peacekeepers in the years ahead during periods of unrest or war, pacifists like you, in times like these. If the world was to end, those who were contacted, people like me, I guessed, would be saved, whisked away from earth to escape the apocalypse. I could only imagine that the get-away vehicles would resemble a fleet of spacecraft like the one I saw when I was eight.

I flashed back to my English professor, Gertrude Herrick, at Westminster Choir College, who told me sometime in the fall of my freshman year, after I must have told her my UFO story one night in her small apartment in Hamilton House (the former dean's residence now being used as a women's dorm) that I wasn't cooperating with the universe. She suggested that I have someone drive me out to the open fields near Princeton, lie flat on the hood of the car, spread my arms wide and look up at the stars, that *they* were trying to contact me. The fields she was referring to were located near Grovers Mills just outside Princeton, the very site of the Martian invasion in Orson Welles' 1938 radio play adaption of H. G. Wells' *War of the Worlds*. I never ventured out to Grovers Mills, in case Gertrude knew something I didn't. After that experience with Professor Herrick, I kept my tales about seeing strange objects in the sky to myself, until Gloria asked.

"Um, maybe these letters look familiar?" I had goosebumps just then, a tingling, but that could have come from a blast of cold air as someone came in from outside.

I'm not sure what I did see that night when I was eight; how the encountered apparition was influenced by my experiences and knowledge of the world up to that point in my life, or why my parents were able to share the same details of it with me the next morning. Did we somehow simultaneously experience a familial collective eidetic hallucination? Or was it some unnamed force or entity that could only be felt yet manifested in my mind drawing upon the technology of the day, the mechanics of flight in the shape of an aircraft, Flash Gordon's rocket made flesh. Or maybe it was swamp gas, we lived across the street from a nearly dried up marshy lake.

At any rate, the workshop proved to be a powerful experience for me. The technique involved spending time in an alpha state, an unfocused loopy place somewhat like a daydream, but more like a trance. Gloria led us in guided fantasies, chanting "every day in every way, I'm getting better and better" and counting backwards from twenty to one interspersed with deep breathing exercises to help us get to alpha. Once we'd become familiar with and knew how to access the alpha state in this manner, she taught us a shortcut on how to get there without the elaborate countdown process. She called it the three-fingers method. While pinching your thumb against the index and middle finger of either hand, and holding them in place, you'd simply breathe in and out three times while counting backwards, 3-2-1. It worked or rather the suggestion worked and once there, we were ushered along mental pathways projecting our minds on, in and through people, mostly strangers we'd never meet. These people were never present in the room and often lived thousands of miles away, all with existing ailments and conditions that we were to diagnose. To validate the diagnosis, another participant always sat beside you holding an index card listing the absent person's name, age, sex and where they lived along with the ailment to be discovered while in alpha. I most always correctly named the problem, the age (within a couple of years) and their gender. It would come to me through a sound, or loosely brushed watercolor images, usually a sky-blue fluctuating shape, almost transparent hovering over the injury. A loud crack with a floating blue line equaled a broken back and the vertebrae affected. An amputated big toe due to diabetes came to me as a black triangle linked by a golden thread connecting the severed digit to where it used to belong on a gnarled foot. During one such exercise, I went a little too deep, a little too far, and had to be retrieved from Alphaland by Gloria. Gloria pulled me back from the darkness and into the light and when I opened my eyes to the glare of the overhead fluorescents, I was still lying on my back flat on the floor, my three fingers pressed firmly together. My participant guide was back in her seat looking concerned as if she had done something wrong, and everyone else just stared at me—*every day in every way, I'm getting better and better.*

Bonfire Embers

IT WAS AS IF JAMES BALDWIN WAS WHISPERING in my ear about the folly in trying to conceal a major part of myself from others by living a supposedly secret life. There was no secret being kept that others couldn't already see through. The people around me had already figured it out or didn't care. They had already accepted me just as I was. A couple of people had tried to ease me out of hiding because, I'd like to believe, they had my best interest at heart.

There were two small events while living and working in Anchorage that remain firm in my mind; people who went out of their way to show me affection, sincere gestures of tenderness and warmth toward another person. I'd like to believe that they were helping me be more my true self because they saw right through my secret. After nearly 50 years I was even able to track down one person, Chris Chalifour, who I knew at St. Mary's, the son of one of the families who worshipped there and who at the time would have been nineteen years old.

There were two Anchorage bars that sat side by side on East Fifth Avenue, the Bonfire Lounge and Embers. The former took up a solitary room, small and nondescript, the Bonfire Lounge catered to a gay clientele. It was so small, in fact, that it didn't need a large following to survive.

The latter was a notorious strip club featuring topless B-girls who spent their time enticing men to buy overly priced, watered-down drinks. For those who were questioning their sexual orientation, the two bars sitting side by side as they were, provided an opportunity for the undecided to spend an evening crisscrossing each establishment's threshold as a test to determine which side they felt most comfortable with, or both, if that made sense, too. Or their proximity to each other provided a justifiable alibi should someone accidentally discover you where you shouldn't be—"Oh, this isn't Embers? That's where I thought I was. It's next door? My mistake."

At any rate, I found myself at the Bonfire one night with Chris. We drove together and parked downtown on East Fifth and walked along the snow-packed sidewalk into the Bonfire Lounge. I had to hold my breath crossing that threshold as I passed into this other world. For some reason, crossing that threshold was an admission that I was gay, if not out loud to those around me, at least silently to myself. For a year after I returned from Alaska and was living at the Jersey Shore, I found myself doing the same thing whenever I entered the M & K or Odyssey, two Asbury Park gay discos. It was like the superstition of holding your breath when passing a cemetery because if you didn't, you'd be the next to die, or in this case the next one to be outed. It was a survival reflex. There was one exception, however, and that was a small piano bar, the Blue Note, which was across the street from the police station in this New Jersey coastal city. Cops would even hang out in the entrance when night court was in session above us on the second floor. Maybe it was singing show tunes and old standards that made it feel all right for me to be there, it was more about the music than just being there to cruise the crowd for someone to take home.

Once inside the Bonfire, Chris and I grabbed a table that was so tiny it forced us to jam our knees together; a hidden intimacy under the cover of tabletops to reach our drinks.

We sat for a while, Chris seemed very open in the comfort of the intimate space and for the time being, I also felt warm, cozy, and safe. He carried the conversation that night. I skirted any discussion of my sexuality, keeping my wall safely in place. I look back now thinking how much I missed out on building an authentic friendship with Chris, a misstep on a journey toward wholeness, if I could have only been true to myself.

We downed our second round of drinks and headed back out into the cold, but instead of heading out of town, we wandered next door to Embers. In our recent exchange of text messages and emails to uncover the details of our night out together, Chris said, in addition to having a crush on me, that it was probably his suggestion to duck into this bar to redeem himself just in case I happened to be straight. He thought that what I would discover once inside would be a turn on for me.

The place had a different vibe from the Bonfire. Here a rowdier, more boisterous crew manned the bar stools and tables. This place was packed. Our table choice was limited to just one by the door with minimal protection from the outside cold anytime someone came in or out of the bar. I kept my jacket on, needing to warm up before I'd take it off. The girls waiting tables on the other hand, braved the frequent frigid blasts of bitter cold air in nothing more than soiled miniskirts and scuffed high heels, topless against the elements, evidenced by their ever-erect nipples throughout the night. They all looked like they could use a good meal rather than serving the sexual appetites of the men who came to tease, heckle, or cop a feel. I felt bad for them, I still do. The only other bar I'd ever been in that seemed to resemble this place and left me feeling creepily uncomfortable was sometime in the late 1980s at a seedy Acapulco drag lounge where skinny queens sloppily lip synched to Dianna Ross and the Supremes while not quite cute servers catered to straight gringo newlyweds and random German tourists. Once I got back to church after my night out with Chris, the only thing I wanted to do was to lock myself in the St. Mary's men's room adjacent to my closet and wash off my smoke-soaked skin and somehow forget the images of those poor girls.

The night out at Bonfire and Embers didn't rekindle my earlier out and proud stance I had prior to arriving in Anchorage. I did feel better, however, with the understanding that I'd take my time to re-out myself when I was ready. If I did, I knew I had others around me that would be accepting. I was weighing my options while completing my alternative service stint. Maybe it had to do with the military's stance on being homosexual, whether in uniform or being a CO, and the accepted views at that time that being gay was a mental disorder. It would've been great if once I came out of the closet, as I had in college, everything else in my life would fall into place. In fact, that wasn't the case for me. That closet door, at least for me, was a revolving one, coming out as if it was the first time whenever I declared who I was to someone new. At the same time there were those who were constantly pushing me back inside, preferring I keep that part of me hidden. Even Chuck Eddy suggested early in our friendship, that it would be best for me to remain celibate, like a cloistered monk. Years later I learned that Chuck had become a powerful straight ally to the LGBTQ community. Nevertheless, in the beginning, at least for me, it seemed an endless cycle of who to trust, who to tell and when to tell them.

* * *

THE SECOND INCIDENT LASTED ONLY A FEW SECONDS but seemed to carry a deeper level of caring than going to a bar for drinks. Jamie Love, a great guy who reminded me of Arlo Guthrie, established a place called the Open Door Klinic in a house in downtown Anchorage. It targeted young people who flocked to Anchorage in the summer from the Lower 48 or *outside* as he called it, in need of housing. The Klinic also provided narcotic addiction counseling for those who needed it, and it was a safe place where some of my group home kids would hang out after school. It was also a place that I'd visit from time to time. I liked the atmosphere, upbeat and positive with a great group of people who lived there, communally sharing the house. I also liked how everyone pitched in to manage the day-to-day tasks of cleaning, cooking, and supporting each other. Sometimes when I visited, I'd bring over a few of my albums to share—*Jesus Christ Superstar*, *Missa Luba*, *Hair!* and the Beatles' *White Album*.

On this occasion, however, I had probably stopped by the collective to follow up on one of the kids at the boys group home. Sometimes kids would end up at the commune seeking safe harbor with Jamie while trying to sort out their lives. Jamie seemed to know when someone who stumbled into his operation was not quite ready for this kind of freestyle communal living; someone who might need to be somewhere else, someplace safer and with more structure. When Jamie referred someone to us at Alaska Children's Services, we'd follow up with him to let him know how his referral was coping in a new setting. If it was a boy he referred and I was involved, the kid would most likely have ended up with Alice Aiken and her charges at the boys group home where I also worked as a relief counselor. Most kids made smooth transitions, in some cases from being nearly homeless after a family crisis to finding a caring and stable place to call home.

After following up with Jamie, I stopped by the kitchen to discover a guy about my age, in his early twenties, boiling water for tea. He introduced himself to me, another name I've misplaced, and asked if I wanted a cup of tea, which I happily accepted. Sitting at the kitchen table, we engaged in small talk, nothing too personal, probably just about the weather, until he asked about where I was from and what I was doing in Anchorage. I filled him in on all of that and in a stalling moment in the conversation, he reached over and gently touched my cheek. It was such a warm and caring gesture that I let his soft touch linger until I heard the silence in the room and jolted back from his caress to reclaim the conversation. I thought that maybe he saw something in my eyes that provoked him to reach out at that moment. Maybe, I thought, he saw a part of me I wasn't ready to reveal just then. Or he saw a part of me he was comfortable with. The moment may have passed in seconds, but that touch, an overwhelming tenderness, has somehow stayed with me forever. There was nothing sexual about it, just the touch from another human. I could have leaned over the table for a hug but didn't, leaving the encounter like an unfinished sentence.

Fancy Meeting You Here

I WAS DROPPING SOMETHING OFF, PICKING SOMETHING UP at Anchorage Community College. I came into a large square foyer with four sets of doors, north, east, south, and west, where you could enter any door, walk straight across, and exit the building on its opposite side. My path took me to the center of the space. The foyer seemed empty except for someone taller than me entering from the opposite side. There was something familiar in his gait, his height, his weight. Getting closer we recognized each other, although I had to do a double take to be sure of who I was accidentally running into some 4,300 miles from Allentown. It was Paul Priest, a friend, who was also a friend of friends back home. Paul's family owned a classic Allentown department store in the style of Bamberger's in New Jersey and Macy's in New York.

"Buzzy! It's you!"

"Paul, what are you doing here? Wow, ah, how is this possible?"

"It's possible. How are you doing?" Paul moved in for a hug, his long dark brown hair and tailored dress coat wrapping around me, too. He was a cross between a beatnik, very hip, and a wealthy hippie, very cool.

I asked him again. "What are you doing here? This is so strange."

It seemed even stranger when he went on to describe his search for a sacred triangle that purportedly connected at three points—beginning at the great pyramid in Egypt, then reaching skyward to the North Star and ending at an invisible point somewhere in the Chugach Range right outside the city. Anchorage was the chosen terminus of this mystical triangle, and it drew followers from the Lower 48 seeking peace and harmony in what was believed to be the beginning of new world order. Paul was seeking enlightenment, and as strange as it all sounded, I had heard the claim before, especially from others hanging out with Mrs. Betty Duffy at her Original Whole Earth Store. Paul was not alone in his search. I wondered if Gloria Whitehead, the Silva Mind Control workshop facilitator who'd asked if I'd ever encountered a UFO, also knew of the triangle and if any extraterrestrials were involved.

Paul and I met up a few times while he was around, talked of life back home. After he told me about his quest, I thought he should meet Mrs. Duffy (I always called her Mother Duffy), who might be able to introduce him to other likeminded pilgrims searching for triangular enlightenment. Her face was framed in a staticky array of wild white hair, which she said had been like that since being struck by lightning as a child. She ran this combo food-book-head shop operation that spilled out of the back of her house and took up the entire space of her garage. There were open bags of grain and peanuts, almonds, and raisins that patrons took advantage of by sneaking handfuls and eating them as they shopped, leaving a trail of crumbs and discarded shells along the way. I read in some news article where the reporter asked her if she considered the grab-and-go munching of her inventory as shoplifting. She said that she didn't, rather seeing it as an overhead expense. She'd just adjust her prices accordingly based on the volume of snacks the customers consumed while browsing. I think her real purpose in the grab-and-go protocol was in making sure people felt comfortable and had something to nibble on in her store.

I often sat with Mother Duffy for hours, drinking homemade wine, usually dandelion, or cheap jug wines out of stained coffee mugs. She was true to her title of affection, *Mother*, offering comfort, advice, telling stories that cunningly served as fables, each with a moral that seemed to relate directly to something I was feeling, struggling with, or felt doubtful about, especially when it had to do with the war and being a conscientious objector. I'd share with her a growing desire to destroy or burn my draft card like so many other men were doing in the lower forty-eight. Don't know if it would have mattered any more as I was already drafted and in the middle of my alternative service.

When I introduced Paul to her, he fell in love immediately, having discovered a sympathetic ear to listen to his theory of an Alaskan utopia. He loved browsing through her collection of new age books. I wondered if he was hoping to discover a tome that would validate the sacred triangle he was seeking.

Paul stopped by the Poor Wind one Sunday evening, the coffee house I set up with the young adult group at St. Mary's. I took time out to sit with him at one of the checker tablecloth-topped spool tables sipping the spiced heated Tang we served and called Russian Tea. Shortly after that evening, Paul vanished without saying goodbye. One day he's here and then he's not; it was all very mysterious. I didn't see him again, not in Alaska nor when I returned home in the fall of 1972 at the completion of my alternative service. I don't know if he discovered the secrets of his sacred triangle or miraculously ascended to the North Star. Either way, it was nice to see him while he was here. Though his visit was brief, his presence for a little while, brought me a much-needed connection to home.

The Trailer

SOMETIME IN MARCH, BEFORE THE CLOUDS AND COLD DRIZZLE of breakup season would blanket Anchorage and the Chugach Range for what seemed like weeks on end, Chuck said it was okay if I wanted to move out of the closet. Let's be honest, privacy didn't exist around my space in the church basement. Evenings were pretty much my own, except when trustee meetings, adult bible classes, or choir rehearsals were taking place or the nights when the Poor Wind coffee house was open. On those nights when I wasn't needed and the church was in use, I was lucky to have the bed in Alice Aiken's RV or a bunk at one of the vacant residential boys cottages to hide out in for a few hours or the entire night. Having the occasional relief counseling job at Alice's group home also gave me some extra cash to be able to afford a cheap place to live if I wanted to.

* * *

March 13, 1972
Dear Herb,
    Wow! Here it is—another March. I got your letter Saturday.

I found a small trailer to live in—or at least to go to when I'm not at church. It's up in Eagle River about twenty-five miles from the city. It's in the woods and on a lake of sorts. Also, many mountains around. Good for the mind. I'm sharing it with an Army friend believe it or not. He is going through some rough times as he is fed up with the Army-military scene. Maybe being at the trailer will help him. Anyways, we are splitting rent on this thing. I may only stay to the end of March, depending on how I feel then.

I wish you would come up here and leave that "East Coast Scene." Alaska could use a good organist. I could be happy with you here also.

I have started rehearsals on my "rock-funk-folk" mass for Easter. The congregation is excited as am I. They really like the music. It is simple, basically, and fun to sing (modest). I start instrumental rehearsals on it on Wednesday. Piano, electric guitars, drums, conga drums, also hoping for a brass ensemble. I already have two trumpets, a French horn and ta-dah, a TUBA. Campy! to say the least. The Apostles Creed sounds like an old bump and grind song from a burlesque show. Maybe not that bad. I will send you a recording. All in all, I've been very productive—one mass and some ideas for anthems, etc. I feel good about the whole thing. Only wish you could be here too.

It's snowing today after around 30 days of pure blue skies and sunshine.

There was a moose last night outside my trailer. I think eating it. It was a cow and stood taller than the neighbor's minibus. A legitimate monster!

My parents move into this townhouse tomorrow or Wednesday. It's going to be nice for them. Mitchell, my younger brother will be off to Goddard College next month. He should be in for a fantastic experience.

Well, write back soon. Like right away. I miss hearing from you. Peace.

Love,

Buzzy

Continue sending your letters to the church address as I am here most often. Trailer is only temporary for the time being.

* * *

IT JUST SO HAPPENED THAT A YOUNG GI, Kevin Taylor, stationed at Ft. Richardson, started attending St. Mary's. He was an administrative aide, on noncombatant duty for the time being. He was a nice guy and we struck up a friendship quickly. We talked about sharing a space after one Sunday's church service.

I had discovered or was told about, can't remember, a small house trailer for rent in Eagle River. I drove up to look. It turned out to be a narrow rectangular structure that had seen better days. It looked like it was from the 1950s and had made the journey north a while ago and now sat on a wooded lot looking abandoned. There was a For Rent sign taped to the door.

It was a simple layout. Walking through the one and only door led you straight into a living area with vinyl bench seating which concealed a bit of storage under the cushions, a small, hinged table that could be lifted for meals, and a tiny galley kitchen in the hallway that took you past a tiny closet-sized bathroom and into a small bedroom with a double bed. There were built in cubbies for clothes or maybe to hold a few books, but nothing more.

I walked around the outside of the structure to check on its condition. This was no sleek and shiny Airstream. It had sat here for several years on cinder blocks, the tires long since removed, a patina of mud, highway salt and time had made it difficult to determine its original color. A fringe of tarpaper hung over the edge of the entire roof indicating that the original one had been replaced or rigged up to better accommodate the Alaska weather.

Sunday rolled around and I saw Kevin after the ten o'clock service. He had taken the stairs up to the choir loft as I was putting away the morning's music.

"Kevin, it's good to see you and I think I found us a place to share if you're interested. It's in Eagle River, about a thirty-minute drive. I've already seen it."

"Really? Ah, what's it like?"

"It's a small house trailer, probably towed up from the Lower 48 a while ago. Nothing fancy, but it has a double bed, small cooking area. It's right off the Glenn Highway, great views of the mountains and it's cheap."

"I'd like to see it, too."

I finished straightening up the choir loft, stacking hymnals and collecting left behind church programs and then I took off for the short ride to the trailer for a second time, this time with Kevin. We met the service station owner and asked if we could look at the place.

* * *

March 17, 1972
Dear Herb,

From this small trailer I am in I have a beautiful view of the mountains. We've had some snow, and everything is beautiful.

The person I am sharing this place with is very much afraid. He is unhappy with the Army. In fact, he is at his limit of tolerance I am afraid. It is sometimes hard for me here with him as I don't know how to help him. Also, his background is very difficult. At 13 he started a two-year affair with his priest. At 16, after his family found out about it, he joined the Army. You can read in all the problems and emotions I'm sure without me going into them now. He is eighteen now—confused, homesick and misses the priest (who lost his wife—divorce—after the incident). I was able to locate his priest for him as I have access to all the priests' addresses, etc. He had to move after the incident—such is life. The Army is very bad (hard) on the boy. Hope he makes it; he has two years left.

Seeing him and being with him makes me wish we were together and not separated. Damn government and social shit.

My mass is going well. Parts, like Kyrie, are hard rock. Opening hymn, Jesus Christ Is Risen Today, is done with brass fanfare, then hard rock drum "introit" and then the hymn—very slow with drums very loud and did I say hard rock. I wish you or my parents could hear it. I keep asking them, but I guess it's hard to get up here. More later on this.

Well, spring should be here in a couple of months. Summer is neat. And it should be fantastic if you can make it up here for a visit.

I think of you every day as you know. I wish I knew when we will be together—later.

Love,
Buzzy

Kevin's heartbreak over his severed relationship with the priest was something I was willing to talk with him about, maybe helping him heal. As for the priest, I was angered that he put Kevin and his family through this ordeal as well as the priest's own family. He had taken advantage of a vulnerable young man, thinking little of his future. Maybe in providing Kevin with the priest's location, he could find some closure to what had happened. I doubted that the information I found on the priest's whereabouts was current, and based on what had happened, whether he had already been defrocked and was in hiding or reinventing himself in some unknown location.

* * *

KEVIN'S AND MY WORK SITUATIONS MEANT THAT NEITHER one
of us could stay in the place every night. I had to be at the boys'
group home at least two nights a week and Kevin was required
to stay on the army base four nights, Monday through Thursday,
while he was on duty. The trailer would function more as a get-
away place, not a permanent residence for either one of us. Since
there'd be no lease, we could rent it by the month. We decided to
give it a trial run for one month, maybe having Kevin as a roommate would help combat some of the loneliness we were both
experiencing. Since we both slept where we worked, me in a closet
and Kevin on base, we'd be able to play house a few days a week
in our own place. If it worked out, well then fine; if not, at least
we had explored living together, even if temporarily. I already had
a couple sets of bed sheets, bath towels and few other household
necessities from when I had my apartment on M Street in downtown Anchorage, so we didn't have to lay out any cash for basic
household goods.

There was only one double bed, we needed to talk about sharing
it together. It wasn't too much of a big deal as there would be nights
when only one of us was sleeping there. I didn't mind the idea of
sharing a bed with Kevin as he was kind of cute. He didn't seem
to mind the arrangement either. Maybe there could be something
between us if we both weren't so buried in what we believed were
lasting relationships outside of Alaska, me and Herb and Kevin
and his priest.

The trailer smelled stale and damp, a little musty with a hint
of gasoline. We spent time scrubbing down the galley kitchen and
bathroom. Swept the place clean, grabbed a couple of beers and ate
sandwiches for supper. Kevin and I spent the evening talking about
where we were from (he was from Phoenix) and what our families
were like. We seemed to enjoy each other's company. The talk was
honest. His life story was far darker than mine; in fact, after listening to him, I felt good about my childhood and college years with
my family.

While we both acknowledged that we were queer, it wasn't something that we spent a lot of time discussing, except perhaps about how Kevin ended up in the Army. Both of us were aware of the fact that the government didn't permit homosexuals serving in its military: if you had a same sex attraction you were to check that little box when you enlisted or were drafted indicating as such; or if you were discovered to be gay while serving, you'd be dishonorably discharged. The view that homosexuality was a psychological malady and regarded as a mental illness would linger until 1973, when the American Psychiatric Association dropped the diagnosis from its list of disorders. I needed to keep my queerness quiet until I was at least done with my two years of alternative service. Kevin would need to do the same. Either way, we were both dealing with elements of loneliness, and probably were looking for a friend we could share some time with, someone separate from our work environments. Someone safe to confide in. We made a strange pair when you consider he was military and I was a conscientious objector, but these differences were never an issue between us.

We cleaned up and decided it was time for bed. I took the right side and Kevin the left. We talked a bit more and then Kevin drifted off to sleep, I listened as his breathing softened and finally drifted off myself.

Maybe ten minutes later I woke up to Kevin crying. I reached over to touch him, to calm him. He was awake. He said he was missing his family, his home and asked if I'd hold him a while. I turned toward him, reached around his chest, and just held on. He reached around my shoulder with his right arm and my waist with his left. We lay like that until he went back to sleep.

We often touched when spending the night together in the trailer, showing affection but never anything more. It was the closest I came to being physically intimate with someone else while I lived in Alaska. We never had sex, I didn't want to push it, although at times it was frustrating. He may have felt the same as me, but didn't pursue it any further either, our intimacy limited to the occasional cuddle late at night.

* * *

April 4, 1972
Dear Herbie,

Well Easter is over. My mass was very successful. My whole day was busy. There were three services at St. Mary's—8, 9 & 11—plus I took a brass group over to St. John's Methodist. Also, I was offered a job to do a sunrise service on top of a mountain, couldn't do that.

Last year when Father Ian Mitchell (the activist priest who composed the American Folk Song Mass, a blending of American folk music styles in a liturgical setting) came to do his mass at Easter, we had 270 people at church. Overcrowded. We can hold 150 and that's crowded. Sunday, we had 397 for my mass. It was unbelievable. All kinds of people, musicians, artists. Tapes came out pretty good—will send you a copy.

I imagine you have been busy with your services and choir tour. What's on?

Weather better here in the 20°s most of the time, somedays in the 30°s. A lot of snow and clouds.

I've run out of money, so I am going to be back at the church. I have an opportunity to house sit at the rectory during one week in April and all of June and July, which gives me a nice big home.

The boy and I together at the trailer seem to be doing more harm than good. I can't seem to help him. I can't even seem to help myself most of the time. It will be better if I am out of there. I think being here together is keeping him from dealing with his reality rather than helping him see it.

*Miss you, please write. Vacation plans? Hope you can
let me know. A good summer.*

Love,
Buzzy

* * *

KEVIN AND I SHARED THAT TRAILER JUST FOR THE MONTH. We ate
a final meal together and a long hug prior to his leaving. I told him
I'd miss him. I never heard from him again. I moved back into my
closet under the stairs at St. Mary's when rent came due.

When I think back to that month living in a rundown trailer
with Kevin, I can't help but wonder if this had become another
missed opportunity for developing a deep relationship with another
person. I whined to myself about feeling lonely and isolated, yet
here was the remedy staring me in the face. We had sought each
other out for the same reasons, but in the end neither of us permitted ourselves to experience something more intimate and loving.
Something we both deserved.

Convocation

By the end of April, I was busy preparing for convocation. All the priests from the state were in town, plus the Bishop of Alaska. We also had the Bishops of Eastern Oregon and Southern Virginia participating as well. On Friday night, April 23, I played the ordination service at All Saints Episcopal in downtown Anchorage. I had been given the list of hymns for the service a week before on Saturday, so I felt confident in being able to deliver a well-rehearsed performance. Not being a church organist, but rather a functional pianist, required me to over practice each hymn, introit, anthem, and mass setting to mask my lack of training.

I was seated at the organ, ready to begin a prelude when the bishop walked over to me and handed me a list of new hymns that he wanted for tonight. All the hymns were different and most I had never played before (I wanted to remind him that I was not even an organist, just a piano player). My nerves were already playing with my head, and now threatened to take control of my hands and fingers, which weren't at all familiar with these new hymns. I was a bit miffed with these last-minute changes to the program. There was nothing else to do but muddle through as best I could and try not to disrupt the solemnity of the event with my mediocre skills on the organ. I would have benefitted with more time to practice so that my fingers had a chance to develop some muscle memory for each hymn. I wanted to play well, both technically and artfully, and in a manner that was befitting to the occasion. I somehow got through the service, with the exuberant voices of the celebrants, local and visiting choirs, and the congregants concealing any missed notes or limping cadences I may have produced.

I found redemption, though, the Saturday night at the final celebration which was held at St. Mary's. I was in charge of music for the entire service, so we did a folk mass and the Bishop, William Gordon, gave the sermon.

Bill Gordon was elected third bishop of Alaska in 1948, and at the age of twenty-nine, the youngest Episcopal bishop in the country. Prior to that he was the missionary and priest serving Arctic coastal villages, including St. Thomas in Point Hope. Twenty years later in 1968, Bishop Gordon convened a gathering of priests and vestry elders in Ft. Yukon to promote and encourage local villagers to manage their own churches. Gordon began ordaining more Alaskan Natives than ever before, twenty-seven in total, to serve as priests in their own communities. This action subsequently led to the reduction in the number of outsiders, white men, who usually served as missionaries in these remote locations. He also was an outspoken supporter of Iñupiat traditions of dancing, whaling, and governing.

I had my church choir, various folk singers, and musicians from the Poor Wind coffee house, along with anyone else who wanted to sing, bring a guitar or banjo, and join our group. The Bishop of Eastern Oregon joined us, too, in the area we carved out for ourselves at the side of the chancel. We also had an Iñupiat choir made up of singers from Episcopal missions from across the North Slope and Northwestern coast. *How Great Thou Art* sung in Iñupiatun, for me, was the musical highlight of that night. Their sound was pure, straightforward, and unembellished, voices that could touch your soul.

People were dancing, hugging, and crying—intimate acts in an overcrowded room. When it came time to *pass the peace*, everyone embraced each other and began shouting, "peace be with you," as the words rumbled across the pews and reverberated throughout the sanctuary. This was nothing like the more reserved handshake and whispered call and response heard at a typical Sunday service.

When all was sung and done, Bishop Gordon found me in the parish hall with a cup of coffee in one hand and a cookie in the other. He had his hand out in greeting. I glanced at the coffee and cookie and gave him a smile and a shrug instead. He asked if I'd be willing to take some time this coming summer and spend a few weeks in the Arctic working with choirs and such. He said it would be in the small Alaska Native whaling village of Point Hope. That sounded wonderful to me and told him that I was interested. This would be a new Alaskan adventure in a part of the state that I knew very little. He thanked me for my help in bringing the music together for tonight's mass as well as for the ordination service the night before. By then, I had found a windowsill to set down my coffee and half-eaten cookie. He grabbed my hand and gave me a hug and moved back into the crowd.

I had heard numerous stories about Bill Gordon from Father Eddy, other priests, and congregants. I knew, when he was younger, he had logged thousands of miles traveling by boat and dog sled to remote villages, both as missionary and priest, and later as bishop. Covering these remote villages in this fashion consumed enormous amounts of time and energy and because of that Bill decided he would learn how to fly. This gave him the ability to better reach and tend to his flock. While flying brought him closer to his worshippers in less time, it also held an unwelcome side effect. Bill had a reputation for crashing, at least six times I was told, not to mention overshooting runways, or taxiing accidentally into the Yukon River. He seemed put off when he had to wait for the weather conditions to improve before taking off and would frequently ignore weight limitations for both passengers and cargo. I learned this during the convocation of the diocese when a collection was taken among the various priests and parishes to purchase an emergency position-indicating radio beacon for the bishop. They seemed to smile, laugh and joke about this, but I took it more seriously, having flown a few times in a small plane with a pilot friend who worked for the FAA, and who'd ask me each time to be on the lookout for emergency landing sites, crash sites he called them, as we flew over rough terrain like Mt. Redoubt, a volcano in the Aleutian Range, or above the Valley of Ten Thousand Smokes in Katmai National Park. It was almost impossible to find a spot suitable for landing, which only added to my stress during these supposedly pleasurable flights. I wondered how effective a transmitter would be when crashed hundreds of miles from anywhere. Would a battery-generated distress signal last long enough for anyone to find a downed bishop and what remained of his plane? I wondered if I would have to fly with Bill Gordon in his plane to reach Pt. Hope.

Bill was a charismatic and socially aware priest and a daredevil bush pilot, rugged, his white hair matching his cleric's collar. He was fearless, compassionate, wise, and loved by the people he served. I recently learned that Bill, who had fully retired in 1986, died in Michigan in 1994. He was buried in Point Hope, the small Iñupiat village he loved, his grave marked by enormous whale jaw bones reaching into the sky, an honor reserved only for the village's most heroic whalers.

Questioning the Presence of God

He said something to me
about words, that each is a name,
and that every name is God's. I who have
no god sat in the vast emptiness silent
as I could be.

—Sam Hamill *The Gift of Tongues*

MY RANDOM RELIGIOUS UPBRINGING HAD FINALLY caught up with me. As a child I attended an austere Congregational church with my grandmother in Lunenburg. Grammy somehow thought I was a holy child and got me a monthly subscription to an Oral Roberts' magazine for children. Roberts, a Choctaw televangelist, had a worldwide following. She took me to my first Wonder Bread and Welch's grape juice communion, an event that only happened four times a year at this local Congregational church, most Sundays intended for preaching the Word. The bread was served on silver-plated platters passed down each pew where every person took a piece and held it patiently in their palms until everyone in the congregation received theirs. The grape juice followed in a similar serving tray but equipped with slots to hold tiny individual cups filled with the purple liquid. Once everyone was served, and as if on cue, the entire congregation popped the small squares of bread in their mouths, chewed and swallowed and then drank the juice from the tiny glass cups in unison; like men at some corner tavern nibbling on bar nuts then in unison downing shots of bourbon that had been lined up and waiting along the bar top. When everyone had finished, the tiny glasses were inserted in drilled out holes in a small wooden shelf screwed to the back of the pew in front of them. I joined the others in drinking the juice, but forewent eating the cubed piece of bread, instead squeezing it in my small fist, holding it there until the service ended. Outside, I tossed the now pulpy lump behind a shrub near the steps of the church. I was afraid that if I ate it, Jesus would pop out of my mouth on the ride home in my grandmother's black '48 Chevrolet *Fleetline*. I still think about that piece of bread every time I pass the church on my way to North Cemetery to visit the family plot or attend a relative's funeral.

I remember the words of Mary Baker Eddy in a Chicago Christian Science church sometime in high school where mind over matter was always a featured topic and wondering if in that approach, I could avoid a visit to the dentist and heal a cavity through faith alone. In July of 1970, as I was waiting for my draft status appeals and doing *La Mancha* at Dorney Park, I'd wear a small silver Star of David medallion on a silver chain, thinking this all made sense. Maybe it had to do with the fact that during that summer I also worked as a camp counselor leading a group of fourth graders in the weekly Oneg Shabbat on Fridays at a Jewish day camp on the side of South Mountain near Allentown—*Baruch Atah Adonai, Eloheinu Melech haolam . . .*

The more I thought about or got involved in religion, the more confused I became, but that confusion never prevented me from self-inducing a luminous, da Vinci-like holographic vision of the Last Supper and having it acted out on the altar of St. Mary's on those nights when I'd have the sanctuary all to myself. Sitting in the first pew in a numinous trance, I'd watch the mystery play out before my eyes, at times I could almost make out the words of these robed apparitions and smell a faint mustiness of a long-shuttered room.

While my personal religious beliefs and spirituality morphed over time as I pondered how and what I believed, I couldn't help but question, in a similar fashion, how each human era sponsored its own cast of supporting deities which seemed to change with each crumbling empire as it relinquished its power to the next. Zeus to Jupiter, Eros to Cupid, same gods, different names until polytheism met monotheism and pagan gods became saints. I began to see it all, including my current belief in Christianity, as mere myth.

Mary Eddy, Chuck Eddy's wife at St. Mary's, had gifted me *You Are the World* by Jiddu Krishnamurti for my twenty-fourth birthday. Based on Krishnamurti's words in my "search for that which is beyond all measure, all time, I'd been caught, trapped, deceived, because I always hoped to find something which is not entirely of this world." Still, I searched for any path that made sense to me, that would lead me to a better understanding of that Divine Mystery. While I searched, I also doubted whether I would ever uncover what it was that I was looking for, yet in that doubt, according to Krishnamurti, I would discover an "energy, vitality, passion to find out."

Regardless of my never-ending inner struggle with all of this, I still marveled at the trappings of the church, the living theater, the robes, processions, music, incense and candles, the ritual, the community that gathered during celebrations. When in Manhattan, whether as a student at Westminster Choir College when we were performing at Lincoln Center or Carnegie Hall or later, after I returned from Alaska, when I was an accompanist for Martha Graham and Alvin Ailey, I would make a deliberate effort to catch a mass at the Church of St. Mary the Virgin or, as it was affectionately known to those of a certain ilk, Smoky Mary's. A service there was akin to attending a Wednesday matinee on Broadway complete with special effects. The singing, both in the pews and the choir loft above, was littered with the voices of chorus boys and girls from nearby hit musicals. It was perfection. Some days the incense smoke was so thick, that if you were seated near the rear of the nave, you could hardly make out the officiants at the altar. On more than one occasion when I was there, the frankincense-filled thurible itself would ignite, spontaneously combusting from its own draft as it swung back and forth on ornate chains, bringing added pyrotechnics to the celebration. I loved it, still do, the pomp and circumstance of it all.

Back at St. Mary's in Anchorage, sometime in the spring of 1972, I joined Father Eddy and a few parishioners in offering a lay-ing on of hands for one of my choir members, Nancy, a woman in her forties who reminded me a little of Gladys Kravitz, Samantha and Darrin's nosey neighbor on *Bewitched*. Nancy had been diag-nosed with terminal cancer. The laying on of hands was used in several sacramental rites from baptism to ordination, and in this case, for healing. She had already spent significant time in the hos-pital and at this point had been sent home until she needed further end-of-life care. We gathered in front of the altar; Nancy seated in a chair. We surrounded her as Chuck explained what we were to do. We placed our hands on Nancy's shoulders and head as Chuck offered his word of prayerful healing. It was a powerful act, and while Nancy was visibly frightened by her diagnosis, we could feel a subtle release in her body, a letting go as she gave in to the sacra-ment. As the moment passed and we withdrew our hands, tears fell from all eyes. We left in silence. Nancy died a week later.

The next day I met with Chuck for our weekly talk. I told him how moved I was by the laying on of hands ceremony the day before and thought that we had brought some sense of peace and comfort to Nancy. I also brought up the topic of eternal life, death itself not the final act in our existence. I struggled during our con-versation, I wanted so deeply to believe in an everlasting life, of a glorious eternity in a heavenly realm. For all I tried, I couldn't wrap my head around it. It made no sense. I lacked faith.

"Chuck, please help me here. I'm seeing no guarantees in any of this. When we die, we die. Tell me, am I wrong? I don't want to be wrong." I wanted to be assured that there was something else, something better after this life. I wanted to be able to assuredly state, "O death, where is thy sting now?"

Chuck was silent for longer than usual when responding to one of my statements or questions during our weekly sessions. He shifted in his office chair and turned to me, the Chugach Mountains framing him through the window over his desk.

"If you're asking if I can guarantee to you that there indeed is life after death, then I should tell you that I cannot. There are no guarantees."

I sat there, not necessarily disappointed in the answer, yet not thrilled either. I was, however, reassured by his honesty with me. His ability to speak to me without plagiarizing a tenet based on church teaching as might be the case with someone other than Chuck.

Then he offered me his own special namaste, something that I was not expecting at the end of our talk, but something I carry with me still.

"Let me say this to you, as I think you're also venturing into an area about faith in God. If you're questioning the presence of God in our lives, in all that is around us, I'd say for you to turn toward someone near, turn toward me now, and when you look at me, look into my eyes and I'll look into yours, know that I'm seeing the Christ in you as you're seeing the Christ in me. Do that and don't worry about the guarantees."

I left his office needing some time alone, some time to ponder his remarks. Then I remembered my mother's teaching from when I was a child, that we each carried a piece of God within us, a spark of the divine. It's in you and it's in me; it's in all living things. I think my mother also saw it in inanimate objects as well and all the time in nature. As someone who was always searching for God in the many churches I attended, flirted with Judaism both in high school and during a brief period as an adult, something clicked for me just then thinking about my mother's and Chuck's words. I felt somehow better, more whole, less agitated or needing to demand answers about the presence of God from others or by belonging to an institutionalized religion, where, as a gay man, I was not always welcome. I could just be, in this moment and in this place.

The sentiment was reinforced years later in 2006. As a high school principal, I often sought out smaller alternative gatherings and workshops that dealt with building meaningful communities, whether in neighborhoods, schools, or corporations, rather than attending the larger conferences and conventions for educators and school leaders. At one such event offered by the Bali Institute for Global Renewal, one hundred attendees gathered outside an old temple compound now serving as an art museum. Archbishop Desmond Tutu was among us and gave what he said was his one and only sermon, one based on the tenets of human rights. He said he'd given it hundreds of times before. He did add, however, that he felt that more needed to be done for the civil rights of LGBTQ people throughout the world. I was impressed that he made that statement and that I was there to hear it, especially since we were in Indonesia, a nation known for its intolerance toward gay people. He ended his remarks by saying that with so many pretty people here, we should all go dancing and with that said, the afternoon's activities came to an end, and we all went dancing.

Later that day I was asked to escort an older woman to a small gathering of the institute's founders for cocktails and dinner at a lush tropical hotel hanging off a cliff which looked out over tiered rice paddies and waterfalls. The woman had slipped and fallen earlier in the day on the polished floor of the old temple turned museum. She asked if I would help her in and out of the hired van or when moving between rooms at the event as a precaution. As the evening progressed, and sometime after cocktails and before dinner, I found myself sitting alone on a tapestried couch surrounded by Balinese art and sculpture. It was nice to have this quiet time away from the reception's chatter. Then, Desmond Tutu came into the room and asked if I minded if he sat down beside me. He, too, was looking for a quiet place to rest before the meal. He had changed out of his gray t-shirt which he'd worn most of the day into a button-up splashed with swirls of wild colors. He still wore his trademark cap: charcoal gray wool with woven braid fastened across the band above the short brim. It resembled a modified cadet cap, squat and with a flattened crown and reminded me of the one once worn by Chairman Mao.

I told him how much I appreciated his remarks that afternoon. I told him I was a high school principal who was gay and out to his students, faculty, school board and community. We talked awhile longer and were interrupted by distant chimes signaling that it was time to make our way to dinner. Desmond leaned over and took my hand in his and said, "You are carrying God within you, and I am carrying God within me, and because we all carry God within us, we are special people, and it's important that we act that way. Please continue to do the work that you do, we need it now in the world more than ever."

The Invitation

I sit on a man's back, choking him and making him carry me, and yet assure myself and others that I am very sorry for him and wish to ease his lot by all possible means—except by getting off his back.

—Leo Tolstoy *What Is to Be Done?*

NO MATTER WHERE I STOOD, THE sea surrounded me on three sides. If I looked west out toward the point and over the weathered mounds of sod houses from earlier times, I could see the Chukchi Sea, a southern portion of the Arctic Ocean; if I looked north or south, it was the same. Only west permitted me a view past the small village, across its tiny landing strip bordered by World War II tank tread marks fossilized in the tundra, around stacks of rusting oil drums and out toward the isolated cemetery—a burying ground fenced in with hundreds of jawbones and ribs of bowhead whales with the largest jawbones jutting up and over heroic whalers' graves. Once past the cemetery, and Marryat Inlet, the tundra's moist blanket of mosses and Arctic willow crept across the permafrost barely anchored in a thin layer of soil.

It was early in the summer of 1972, four months before the end of my two years of service, when I received a letter from Fairbanks. The return address proclaimed it to be from The Right Reverend William J. Gordon, Bishop of Alaska. The bishop had asked me earlier that spring if I'd be willing to help with music in one of the Episcopal outposts scattered throughout the state. The missive I held in my hand was the official invitation to take on an extended assignment in the remote Iñupiaq whaling village of Point Hope 125 miles above the Arctic circle. Bishop Gordon wanted me to work with the singing groups of St. Thomas, an Episcopal mission, and train one or two people on the church's small organ.

The bishop was familiar with my work at St. Mary's, having celebrated mass and confirmed congregants twice during the time I served as the church's choir director and organist. He had even asked me to play for an ordination service for new priests at All Saints Episcopal Church, the area's *mother church* in downtown Anchorage, during a diocese wide convocation of clergy and lay representatives. The invitation, although anticipated after talking to the bishop during convocation in April, still came as a surprise and an offer that I willingly accepted. I felt empowered, both as a CO and musician, to have been given this unique opportunity. This project gave me a renewed sense of purpose and a chance to use my training as a musician in a new setting. It reaffirmed for me that I was functioning as the kind of conscientious objector I had crafted in my mind. I was serving others through a means that I felt capable of, passionate about and that I wouldn't shy away from. As I began to prepare for my stay in the Arctic, I noticed that some of the loneliness and isolation that had been my constant companions during my time as a CO began to diminish. There was something about this project at play within me that countered the effects these demons had on me. Maybe it had to do with the alignment of my passion for music with the purposeful sharing of it with others and the challenge posed by the remote location where it would all come together.

A few weeks later, I boarded a Wein Consolidated 737 combi at Anchorage International for a direct flight to Nome. The plane's dual purpose was evident as soon I crossed the tarmac and climbed the mobile boarding stairs to the plane. To the right of the main cabin door along the fuselage, a large cargo door gaped wide like an open mouth swallowing crates filled with supplies and machinery destined for remote outposts throughout the state. As I moved inside, I noticed that a few rows of easily removable seats had been added for passengers who sat just in front of the soon-to-be-tethered payload.

Landing at Nome with its massive birchwood hangars, I had enough time for a walk around this gold rush outpost before boarding my next flight, a single-engine bush plane that would get me to Kotzebue for a two-night layover in a small coastal village. Once off the plane I gathered my belongings, my duffle stuffed with clothes and my guitar safely stored in its case. Walking from the landing strip, dragging the duffle at times along the gravel road bordering the bay, I made my way through a maze of shacks and sheds that encroached the narrow path. At water's edge skiffs, some with outboard motors, rested calmly in the water while salmon the color of ripe clementines, gutted and split just up to the tail, straddled elevated horizontal wood poles and cured in the sun.

My only encounter on my walk to the hotel involved dodging a volley of spit from three young men drinking beers, yelling "nigger" and something else, something guttural, I imagined, in Iñupiatun. I froze, turned, and looked at the three. They seemed to freeze, too. I could tell by their body language that they weren't looking to initiate anything like a fight, which I'd be useless in, but rather kept their positions on a makeshift bench; their action not so much a physical threat as a wakeup call sent my way—the *gussuk*, in their territory. I don't know if this would have happened if I were walking with others, but I was alone and weighed down with my baggage, an easy target. Then, as if on a movie set, with the director shouting "action," they returned to whatever they were talking about before I came upon them.

A few minutes later I arrived at the hotel, upset, and wet with sweat, and feeling a mixture of guilt and fear. Had I unwittingly done something to offend these men by just walking along this road? Would I be subjected to this aggression again while I was here? This was my first time in an Alaskan Native village, having spent all my time in Anchorage except for hiking in the mountains or panning for gold at the abandoned Independence Mine or a late-night drive to the Double Muskie Inn in Girdwood southeast of the city. I hadn't experienced any push back for being white, at least not to my face. I was unnerved.

When the Alaska State motto, "North to the Future," was suggested by journalist Richard Peter, and made official during the Alaska Purchase Centennial in 1967, he defended the slogan by saying, it was "a reminder that beyond the horizon of urban clutter there is a Great Land beneath our flag that can provide a new tomorrow for this century's 'huddled masses yearning to be free'". The motto served, even if subtly, as a renewed call (which began when Russia discovered Alaska in 1741), to those in the Lower 48, and across the seas, that this last frontier was where you'd find unbound freedom and possibility even at the cost of exploiting the state's vast resources. According to a 2002 report released by the Alaska Advisory Committee to the U.S. Commission on Civil Rights, the freedom these new huddled masses yearned for came "at the expense of the state's Native people; for, in their zeal to exploit the state's resources, masses of newcomers have consistently failed to recognize and respect the rights of Native Alaskans."

* * *

EVEN THOUGH I HAD BEEN WORKING and living among kids and families from remote Native Alaska villages in Anchorage group homes and shelters for almost two years, it only partially prepared me for what I'd discover about myself and others in Point Hope and this short layover in Kotzebue. I was still, although less so since arriving in Alaska, influenced by stereotypical Eskimo images that began entering mainstream media with the advent of commercial whaling in the form of drawings, etchings, and stories. Robert Peary's historic Arctic explorations of Greenland, spanning more than ten years from 1889-1909, were captured in photographs and shared worldwide in newspapers and periodicals. As a child I may have even seen similar images in the stacks of tattered National Geographic magazines stored in an upstairs bedroom of my grand-parents' house in Fitchburg, Massachusetts or maybe in the pages of our World Book Encyclopedia collection. My understanding of Eskimos was further abstracted in cartoons and movies, which continued to persist throughout my childhood and teen years. These pictures from another time, portrayed a romanticized tradi-tional Inuit lifestyle where villagers only wore animal-skin parkas and mukluks, kissed with their noses, or raced through the tundra on dog sleds hunting polar bears and sailing off in seal-skin skiffs to harpoon whales; two-dimensional depictions a child might pre-fer over the reality of modern-day life in a remote Arctic village. Later, once I finally arrived in Point Hope, the stereotypes took on a physical form that at times looked a lot like those remembered images from my childhood. What I failed to see as a child, was the humanity that lived behind those captured scenes, a humanity, now that I was here in person, I could touch and hold. Breaking down and getting rid of those old stereotypes was easier once I was able to stand among these people, so much easier than removing the one I held onto for myself, the one that others might assign to me if they knew I was gay. I was an outsider standing among a people seen by others as outsiders, exotics. I was now the other, the one who was different, the outsider looking in, the one who would have to adapt to be of use, to fit in, to survive, and yet I felt at home.

Adding to that was the fact that I was raised in a small New England town in North Central Massachusetts where we all looked the same. I went to school in a building where boys and girls lined up and entered through separate doors identified by gender on opposite ends of the schoolhouse. Once inside, we immediately mixed up in hallways only to be rearranged again alphabetically and by rows in the classroom. It was fourth grade sometime in the late spring that my class put on a minstrel show complete with burnt-cork blackface, spirituals, and jokes. I loved the smell of the cork as its gritty charcoal altered my face. Having never met someone of a darker skin color, and never having encountered this kind of diversity in Lunenburg, I only saw this sooty makeup as part of a class project, a musical extravaganza, at the time neither offensive nor something to be questioned. Or was all this a more sinister lesson lurking in some hidden curriculum? Diversity and cultural correctness were not part of my vocabulary as a boy. I was not aware of seeing others as different. Well, maybe except for French Canadians and Irish Catholics, even though I looked like them. These were people my mother disliked for some unknown reason; except I do remember her stating that the Pope would really be governing the United States should John F. Kennedy become president. I loved John Kennedy but didn't let her know.

At the time, I may have missed, and now no longer remember, all the darker elements of institutionalized racism that masqueraded in song, dance, mime, and jokes told in a demeaning dialect; it was too easy a pill for a child to swallow. What I do remember most, however, is the scent of cold cream as I grabbed it by the fistfuls and smeared it on my face to wipe away the black.

* * *

THE LONGER I LIVED IN ALASKA, THE MORE I BECAME AWARE of the toll paid by Alaskan Natives due to outsider expansion, exploration, and exploitation. Smallpox, measles, the Spanish flu, tuberculosis all joined hands with alcoholism in a ring-around-the-rosie circle of death and destruction, leaving a score of unmarked mass graves and ghost towns in its wake. Wave after wave of disease seeped in from the sea, carried ashore on the backs of seamen, missionaries, prospectors, and prostitutes. The invasion continued to make its way inland, a colonizing crawl creeping along Alaska's rivers and up and down its coasts resulting in the widespread loss of life, language, and culture. British, American, Japanese, Russian and others profiting from the abundance of whales along the Alaskan northwest coast further pushed a global commercial agenda spawning shoreline towns speaking unknown tongues and bartering manufactured goods, alcohol and supplies for furs and trinkets. Wave after wave of plagues took their toll, the Alaska Natives lacking the needed immunity to overcome each new onslaught. Entire villages and regions were decimated during the Great Sickness of 1900 following the discovery of gold in Nome in 1898.

In Anchorage I had seen first-hand the lingering aftermath of this invasion when I'd don protective clothing and face mask in order to safely accompany one of the boys from the group home to visit his infected father as he lay struggling to breathe in the TB ward of the Alaska Native Hospital; or when wandering downtown along a stretch of derelict bars on Fourth Avenue that catered to a disenfranchised native clientele, unwelcome in the more respected establishments of the city, who hunted only for cheap booze and beer to feed another disease we helped spread: alcoholism.

I attended a funeral for one of these men, the father of one of the boys in my charge, Mike, a lovable 15-year-old Athabaskan native, tall for his age, with a buzzed haircut, polite and quiet. He'd asked Alice and me to go with him. We drove into the city, parked, and walked into the narrow storefront mortuary, which shared space on the block with an evangelical church next door. In fact, I think it was all one enterprise, a door connecting both places at the rear of the building. We took our seats with Mike between us and faced the back wall where his dad rested in a closed unfinished pine box. There were no flowers, only sunlight streaming through the plate glass display windows casting the name of the funeral chapel in shadows on the shoulders of the mourners in front of us. When the preacher stood up to deliver his homily with bible in hand, his words were laced with contempt and tempered by his unearned privilege. All fire and brimstone, he spewed his words of hate, called the deceased a sinner not fit for redemption, a consumer of the devil's brew and evil ways; and looking out to the living in the room, said that there was still time for us to repent, but alas, not for Mike's dad. It was too late for him. He'd lost his chance at redemption. I was appalled with what was going on, how the preacher behaved, how his words stung. I hadn't encountered anything like this in any of the churches I had attended during my life up until then. I reached over to give Mike a shoulder hug and noticed Alice reaching to take his hand.

The preacher called it quits, there were no *amens* from the mourners. He was preparing to exit through the door at the back of the room when a hand went up from someone in the front row to the right of the coffin. Four large women sat side by side wiping tears away. The preacher acknowledged the interruption.

"Yes, what is it?"

The woman, Mike told me it was his aunt, his dad's sister, asked, "Can you read us the Twenty-Third Psalm before you go?"

The minister seemed flustered, annoyed, and with bible in hand uttered, "I don't have that prepared. I don't have that with me." I couldn't believe what I was hearing, the man had the psalm with him, he knew it by heart.

The women, in resigned acceptance of what had just taken place, gathered their belongings, helped each other up from the folding chairs and with eyes cast toward the floor, walked past us and the other mourners and out into the cold. We met them on the sidewalk. Mike introduced us to his aunt and her friends. They reminded me of an aging, slightly overweight female vocal group from the Forties, the Andrew or McGuire Sisters, all standing side by side on the curb. Following the introductions, Alice and I offered to recite the psalm for them, we both had memorized it as children. It was part of my repertoire acquired through exposure to a variety of protestant churches growing up. The seven of us recited it together. After we finished, the women went on their way and we took Mike out to lunch to talk about his dad, the good times, before returning to the group home. This all took place sometime in late winter or maybe early spring as there was no burial that day; the ground still too frozen to dig a grave. Mike would have to wait a while longer to say a final goodbye to his dad.

The whole experience with the preacher angered me. I saw it as a blatant act of discrimination toward this Athabaskan family and all the others in the room.

* * *

THE KOTZEBUE HOTEL WAS A MODEST TWO-STORY well-weathered wooden building facing the bay. Its life on the coast had taken its toll. I had pre-booked a room. It was sparse with two twin beds and a nightstand in between. A little lamp rested atop the nightstand and a small rectangular window, eyebrow-like, sat high on the wall. There were five other guests staying in the hotel that night, a German student enjoying a summer abroad, and a family of four from France traveling with their teenage son and daughter. That night we ate together at a common table in the hotel's dining room. Four languages, English, French, German, and a couple of staff members speaking Iñupiatun, brought an element of confusion and laughter during the meal. We were passing peas to people who had asked for sauce. Potatoes when someone asked for salt. Then we all attended a performance of Iñupiat dancing, drumming and a blanket toss demonstration. A rehearsed presentation geared toward tourists whenever they were in the village, either from the Lower 48 or elsewhere, and offering just a minimal taste of Iñupiaq culture, and it was all included in the price of the room. The performance, while well-executed, seemed a bit stereotypical, offering a mere post-card snapshot of these traditions without providing much detail on their origins. After we returned to the hotel, the German boy joined me in my room where we passed my guitar and a couple of bottles of Budweiser back and forth between us as we shared songs late into the night.

The next morning, I made my way back down the gravel street in search of St. George's in-the-Arctic. I was on edge thinking I'd run into the spitting name-callers from the day before, but they were nowhere to be found. I remained vigilant nevertheless as I walked on. Some part of me almost wanted to run into them again, hoping I'd have the moral courage I'd need to talk with the trio, to learn something about each that could make a difference in our lives.

It had been more than one hundred years since Seward's *folly* of a $7.2 million purchase of the territory in 1867 had ignited the coordinated efforts by the government and various, handpicked Christian denominations to "civilize" the indigenous population. I wondered if the men I encountered the day before saw me as a colonizer, a descendent of those who came before me, with the same mission to indoctrinate them to the American way of life while simultaneously destroying their culture. I considered my alternative service assignment and realized that I had been working with Alaska Children's Services, an organization operated by three different Protestant denominations and where children, once placed in one of our group homes, shelters or residential treatment cottages, were expected to worship Christ following the tenets of the denomination managing that home. Some of our kids were sent away to Bureau of Indian Affairs' boarding schools as part of the government's continuing effort to "civilize" Alaskan Native youth. Now I was headed to St. Thomas Church in Point Hope, one of the first Episcopal missions established in 1890. Were my hands clean? I didn't feel like I was on a mission to change anyone's way of thinking or living. I wasn't here to proselytize or save souls. I was here, however, to share my music with others, to make a difference without causing harm.

I found St. George's in-the-Arctic on a side road between the hotel and airport. I had heard about a rug in front of the altar and wanted to see it. I can't quite remember who might have told me about it, maybe it was Chuck Eddy back at St. Mary's or someone at the Kotzebue hotel. When I approached the altar, the rug turned out to be a large snow-white polar bear skin, its head facing me, glass eyes eternally staring and mouth slightly open baring sharp teeth. It fanned out from the altar running down the two steps between the communion rails which separated the chancel from the nave. If you were to take communion or go up to the altar, it seemed only proper, to me anyway, that in addition to genuflecting to the cross you'd also offer a similar gesture to the bear by respectfully patting its massive head and saying, "peace be with you." I sat in the front pew in awe of the rug's sheer size, its motionless beauty. How had he ended up here? Was he hunted down, or did he wander into Kotzebue during a blizzard, lost in a whiteout and slaughtered by local villagers? I wanted to offer my condolences to the bear or help him find redemption from this place. I returned to the hotel in a contemplative state, a walking meditation on nature and faith, on the relationship between man and beast, the hunter and the hunted, forgiveness and redemption.

I thought about my own redemption as I struggled to come to terms with my homosexuality. It hit me hardest at nineteen years old when I came home for spring break. Two friends, Herbie, my college roommate, and Ara, a friend I met in Princeton, came up for a day to visit me in Allentown. At the time, we lived in an old farmhouse on the side of a hill. Above the house, the hillside provided the three of us with a great place to hike for the afternoon.

While the boys were talking in the living room, I went into the kitchen. My mother began questioning me about what we planned to do while hiking, I think she may have been suggesting that we were going to be getting high, doing drugs. I took her inquiry as an inquisition into my being gay. Something that she had difficulty accepting. I blew up at her, late in realizing that this was not what she was questioning me about at that moment. I lurched into a rant saying something like, "So what if I'm queer, lots of people are this way." I may have even outed a few historical figures like Michelangelo or Da Vinci or who knows, there were not a lot of historic gay role models in print or easily available to me at that time. You often felt like there was no one else in the world who felt or acted the same way you did, at least for me, in the late 1960s. Then it hit me, redemption for being gay was not going to come from an outside source. I wouldn't be absolved by a pastor, church, or religion. My redemption would have to come from within. I needed to redeem myself. I told my mother that it was not my choice to be this way, queer, and that I was not an evil person because of who I was or how I was raised.

My mother and I didn't speak for the rest of the day. She sat alone in a rocking chair in the corner of the living room. I needed to leave the house. Herb agreed to take me back to college, where I stayed for the remainder of spring break. My dad called me later that night. When I answered the third floor pay phone outside my dorm room, he told me I had hurt my mother with my words that day. I told him that I was hurting, too, and that I needed to be alone to work this all out. Three days later I received a care package from home filled with candy bars and Pringles, homemade oatmeal cookies, and a novelty sign printed on glossy card stock that read, *Save Water! Shower With a Friend*. I think it was my mother's way of apologizing and maybe beginning to come to terms with my sexuality.

On my final morning in Kotzebue, I made my way along the shoreline road back to the airport. I boarded an even smaller plane than the one that had brought me here two days before. This one delivered mail to remote settlements along the coast, including Point Hope, my final destination. I'd be there in about an hour, and my time in the sky gave me an opportunity to reflect on the work ahead at St. Thomas—playing church services, working with the choir in learning and performing the mass I composed and teaching guitar and keyboard lessons to anyone who might be interested.

Point Hope

I LEAVE THE BUILDING THAT I TEMPORARILY CALL HOME, an old
single-story bungalow shipped to Point Hope in pieces and
rebuilt, along with the nearby rectory. I've been shown a long and
narrow space, much larger than my closet back in Anchorage,
with a cot and a few hooks to hang my clothes in what might
have once served as a coat closet in this multi-use building—
the church's parish hall and guest house. I walk out across the
spongey thin layer of soil floating above the permafrost toward
the pebbled shore, not very far. There are no trees anywhere for
at least one hundred miles to hinder the way, not until the foot-
hills of the Brooks Range far to the east. I see two lone figures
crouched by the water; each holds an end of seal sinew rope
attached to a hand-drawn seine. One person is throwing beach
stones out past and alongside the open net with her free hand.
As I get closer, I recognize Donald and Lillie Oktalik, the village
Episcopal priest and his wife. They're fishing for Dolly Varden or
anything else that might be chased into the seine by the splashing
stones, hoping something of interest swims within the arc of the
net, so they can carefully pull it closed, drag the catch to shore

and ready it for supper. They'd been sitting there for hours, they tell me, catching nothing.

I turn west and continue walking along the shoreline past the current village and the Nalukataq grounds. Silhouettes of skeletal bowhead whales give witness to where, just days before my arrival in the Iñupiat village of Point Hope, whaling crews and families gathered to mark the end of spring whaling season, when the bounties of the hunt are celebrated and shared with the village amid blanket tosses and feasting. The skin-covered umiaks with their paddles, spears and harpoons used for the kill, are proudly displayed by each crew. My walk takes me farther out on the triangular spit, Tikiġaq, shaped like a slightly curved index finger pointing out into the Chukchi Sea some 125 miles north of the Arctic Circle. I'm on sacred ground.

At times I toe an odd object on the tundra's surface: bone, wood and reindeer antler seine needles, spear heads, harpoon points and pieces of fossilized ivory, walrus vertebrae disks and seal ear bones. I stoop down to collect a few interesting items. I'm told I can do this as long as I don't scavenge beneath the surface of the soil. I'm not to disturb the ancestors or rattle the ghosts and spirits. I find and pocket what appears to be a human finger bone, the color of a pale oyster, it looks too small to be a seal's phalanx.

I pass an *ivrulik* and notice a number of these semi-subterranean sod houses of Old Tigara Village where two old women still live and which border the more recent prefab buildings of Point Hope and worn-out World War II structures, now reclaimed and repurposed for village use.

I go inside one of the abandoned, sod-covered structures. These earthen and whale bone houses seem to rise out of the land then disappear below the surface like a passing pod of whales. They look alive, these creatures burrowing through the soil, their entryways gaping wide like mouths lined with the skeletal remains of bowhead instead of teeth. These beasts of bone, timber and sod try in vain to hold back the ever-encroaching earth and sea as they reclaim their territory, laying waste to them all, driving them below the surface, plowing them out of existence.

I crawl through the structure's long and narrow passage that takes me to an open space, the belly of the beast. A hole in the ceiling allows a ray of sunlight in to chase any shadows into the cracks and crevices in this room—a room where soil seeps through the bone and driftwood walls and spills around platforms once used for sleeping. It smells vaguely sweet. I can hear the Arctic wind blowing across the hole in the roof like a breath passing over the mouthpiece of a flute. The song fills my being, my thoughts, my breath. It's a song without words because words are not needed. It's an old song. I'm inside the whale of Iñupiaq myth, the one about the raven, who, sparked by his curiosity in seeing a whale, flies into its mouth and in the belly discovers a beautiful woman protecting a lamp. The woman warns raven not to touch the lamp, then leaves while raven remains inside the whale. When she returns, she sees that the flame has gone out and, because of that, she dies. Raven then understands what he has done and learns that the woman is the whale's soul, the flame its heart, and her coming and going, the whale's breath.

I crawl back out of the house and walk farther out again toward the tip of the point. I wander around earthen mounds and depressed pits of an even earlier time, the ancient Ipiutak village, some 2,500 years old, discovered by archeologists Helge Larsen and Froelich Rainey in 1939 during their first expedition to Point Hope. I wonder about these ancient people from a previously unheard-of culture living on this fragile spit of land jutting out into the sea and the lives lived in the settlements that followed over thousands of years. There are easier places to call home.

Years later, having lost contact with anyone in Point Hope, I'm seated with a small gathering of people in Ubud, Bali. We're listening to storyteller and environmental writer Barry Lopez share his stories about places he's been, the importance and sacredness of remote communities like Point Hope. He tells a story of an Arctic village. I mention my time in Point Hope more than thirty years earlier. He knows this place and tells me that the village where I stayed is no longer there. I'm saddened by this news, and irritated with myself for not knowing, for forgetting. Like its earlier predecessors, the village could no longer sustain its inhabitants, in this case due to the rising sea level. Lopez says that the new village was built in the mid-1970s on the other side of the landing strip, shortly after my time there. A mini, modern village laid out on a grid. Houses sitting side by side, a school and firehouse, like city blocks intersected by avenues and cross streets. A large wall stretches out across the northern edge of town, a shield from fierce Arctic winds, blowing snow and a hopeful deterrent to wind-fanned flames and embers spreading from house to house in the event of a fire.

I stand on an old beach ridge near the tip of Tikiġaq, staring out across the sea toward the thick fog bank marking the location of the receding polar ice. I may even be standing on the same spot where in 1924, polar explorer and folklorist, Knud Rasmussen, and his two friends, Arnalulunguak and Meetek, stood when they visited Point Hope while navigating the Northwest Passage during Rasmussen's Fifth Thule Expedition, a brutal endeavor to uncover the genesis of the Eskimo *race*. Their journey of more than three years covered 20,000 miles, mostly by dog sled from Baffin Island to Cape Dezhnev in Siberia.

I am speechless and await a new song.

Planet of the Apes

Now I stood where time had no meaning, where the sun circled my days and nights, never quite dipping into the sea. I'd leave my room each morning with my guitar slung over my shoulder and cut across the short distance to St. Thomas, the small Episcopal mission on the northern edge of the village.

There was a one-sentence blurb in the church's one-page bulletin the Sunday prior to my arrival announcing my purpose for being in the village. There was no further communication about it after that, and, I would learn, no need for posting choir rehearsal or music workshop days and times. I wondered how I would attract followers without additional advertising.

"Fifteen minutes before you're ready to begin," said Donald Oktalik, the village patriarch and the St. Thomas's ordained priest, "ring the church bell and see who shows up. They know you're here and want to work with you."

"Just like that?"

"Have faith," was all he said and went back to carving a replacement part out of whale bone for his snowmobile.

I didn't have faith. I was a doubting Thomas working in a

remote Arctic church named after the very same questioning apostle. Nevertheless, ringing the bell worked. Yet, the cause and effect, ring the bell and they will come, did little to bolster my faith that it would happen any time I rang that bell. At any rate, people showed up for these sessions—choir rehearsals, guitar lessons and practice with anyone even minimally interested in playing hymns for services on the temperamental electric organ.

So, I'd pull the rope that rang the bell outside the church door that brought the people that became my students. I also played the weekly church service, and on my last Sunday in Point Hope we performed the folk mass I composed for St. Mary's. On another Sunday when the power had failed, I pulled out the old asthmatic missionary organ, a simple reed instrument with a shortened keyboard and bellows covered in seal skin, the original leather long since worn out and discarded. The power exerted by the bellows was no match for the single rank of tired reeds and no matter how hard I pumped on its hanging pedals, the organ could only wheeze out a barely sustainable tone. Adding chords to the melody compounded the struggle, causing the poor thing to gasp for its next breath of air each time I pumped the bellows. In a demonstration of sincere empathy, the congregation adjusted their singing out of an unexpected sense of compassion and respect for the ailing instrument.

The community went out of its way to make me feel a part of the village, inviting me for suppers of cold canned vegetables and muktuk pulled out of sigulaks, square holes dug into the permafrost which served as ice cellars. Many houses had personal sigulaks where families stored provisions, but there were larger ones, too. Each whaling crew dug deeper vertical shafts accessible by ladders and fortified with wood planks and posts that led below the tundra and provided additional storage space for large amounts of whale meat caught during the hunt. I was told that the spirits of the caught whales also resided in the sigulaks along with the meat, adding a sacred purpose to the space.

The meals I consumed seemed to consist of a combination of metallic mush and rancid blubber. I learned quickly to tilt my head back while chewing the sticks of blubber so that the whale oil could find a path to my stomach while avoiding my taste buds. I may have made a big deal about it at first, using humor to deflect my early discomfort with this new taste experience, but soon I found myself eating and smiling and grateful for being part of their world and having something to eat. Meals became a daily eucharist, sacred and celebratory as we gave thanks to the sacrificed whale whose flesh sustained us.

That night I walked along gravel paths in one of the oldest continually inhabited settlements in North America, passing the corrugated metal clad post office, 99766, and parked dog sleds attached to snowmobiles. I soon arrived at the World War II-era Quonset hut which now served as Point Hope's one and only movie theatre. A screen mounted on one wall faced off against rows of backless benches which, after the first few rows, grew incrementally higher on stilt-like legs. A wobbly balcony offered an unobstructed view to the screen. Weakly anchored to the floor but not to each other, the bleachers seemed to float under the half-moon arc of the structure's corrugated roof. Maintaining balance, particularly at the higher levels, was a team effort. One unexpected movement from any one bench mate could topple the entire colony. A 16 mm projector balanced uneasily on a metal shelf bolted to the back wall. To start, stop or change reels required the use of a stepladder. A single cable slid down the wall beneath the projector and across the floor making its way to a single speaker below the screen. Films were delivered at will from some unknown distributor or library in Nome or Fairbanks on the plane that carried the mail.

The audience arrived with that certain excitement of a night out with friends who haven't seen each other in some time, even though most of them had spent the entire day together. Someone offered me a hand and I was hoisted up onto one of the medium height bleachers. I immediately surrendered to the group's sense of balance as my legs dangled freely below. This simple gesture, a hand reaching out to welcome me, to join these intimate strangers for a couple of hours of Hollywood diversion, meant everything to me at that moment. I had never been so far from home and in need of feeling connected, of being accepted. Yet here I was, at the end of the world, finding that connection, that acceptance. As our row engaged in a perpetual game of give and take to maintain balance, we began to know and trust our places on the bench. We seemed to breathe together, adapting to each other's movements, protecting the whole lest one of us forgets where he was, and we all come tumbling down.

The windowless Quonset provided the perfect remedy to the midnight sun outside. Someone climbed the ladder with this evening's presentation and threaded the first reel of film through the projector. As the film wound its way through the sprockets, the operator motioned for someone in the audience to switch off the lights. Darkness gave way to the film leader's dyslectic numeric countdown, 10, 9, 8, 7, 6, 5, 4 . . . fade to black and then the single monophonic speaker crackled out a snare drum cadence and brass fanfare as searchlights scanned an iconic art deco monument to Twentieth Century Fox, Charlton Heston in *Planet of the Apes*. I struggled to hear any dialogue or follow the plot due to the increasing laughter from the audience, who are finding this epic one of the funniest comedies they had seen. There came a point where I was laughing, too, not understanding what made the film so funny to them, yet somehow caught in a paroxysm of giggles.

The Black Freighter

WHEN I WAS A KID, THE WOODRUFF DAIRY TRUCK would rattle its way down Flat Hill Road twice a week. I could hear the clatter of glass milk bottles as they rattled against wire crates long before the truck leaned into the curve approaching our little neighborhood, an unplanned cluster of discordant houses built on both sides of a tar-covered country road. It was late July. I grabbed my fishing gear and waited by the kitchen door for Paul Woodruff to deliver our milk order and then joined him for the ride further down the road to my grandparents' summer camp. I loved standing next to him in the cab with its sliding doors wide open as he drove the short distance to a string of lakeside cabins. Even with the wind passing through the truck, you could still smell the distinct odor of Paul's farm as we made our way to Lake Shirley.

Grammy stood at the backdoor; well, really, there were only two side doors for this building, one off the bedroom, where she stood waiting, and the other on the screened in porch at the other side of the house and nearer to the lake. There was no front door. A strangely cubist structure trying desperately to resemble a house and pieced together over many years with spaces ill-conceived in my grandfather's imagination and realized in found objects and scrap lumber.

An antlered deer's head jutted out from one wall, the result of a tragic accident one night, or so I was told, when the thing ran across the road and with a desperate leap, crashed through the house, its head sticking through the inside wall, its eyes holding a bewildered gaze as it watches over the room. There was no explanation for what happened to the rear end of the animal. As a kid I thought it would have jutted out from the side of the house just under the eaves based on how he told the story. My grandfather told great tales and some of them were even true.

The plumbing was purely an afterthought with pipes like horizontal buttresses running alongside the outside clapboard walls of the cottage and providing water to the kitchen sink. That's as far as the indoor access to water went. There was no bathroom only a two-hole outhouse set some distance away, which seemed like an endless journey to get to in the middle of the night.

I got my hug from Grammy as Grampy raised the flag and pledged allegiance to it, his daily ritual beside the lake. The clanking of the rope and pulley sending chickadees scurrying for cover in the brambles, white birches, and pine trees nearby. At the edge of the dock, I dropped my line into the dark lake water, morning sun and sky reflecting on its surface.

I caught a yellow perch that morning, nothing to brag about, too small for a proper fish tale, but just right for a boy's breakfast. Bringing it to Grammy, she took the morning's catch and with a simple kitchen knife delicately scraped away its scales, sending them into the swill bucket beside the sink. On the wood counter, she deftly filleted the small creature removing spine, fins, head, tail, and guts in what seemed like one smooth and uninterrupted motion. Wiping her hands on a soiled apron, she reached for the cast iron skillet, dropping reserved bacon fat from a greasy jar, the remains of an earlier meal, and set the pan on an already lit kerosene stove. The smell of fish, fat and fumes filled my lungs.

Nothing spoken between us as she cooked, a silent meditation of sorts, punctuated with small smiles as she made my breakfast.

Eagerly taking a seat at the dining table and facing the poor dead deer's head, I ate the meal put before me, a small fried perch with toasted Finnish coffee bread served on blue Arabia china. I ate as she watched, bright blue eyes the same color as these cherished plates, an immigrant's dowry brought from Finland in 1908.

I'd overheard my mother and Aunt Martha quietly talking about where my grandmother came from, like it was a secret. Not that being from Finland was a secret, but where she was from in Finland. She was from Ylitornio, a small town that for a while bounced between being part of Sweden or Finland depending how the border shifted or politics shaped the region, which they called Lapland. My mother and her sister would often refer to an oil painting that hung in my grandparents' other house, the house they lived in once summer was over and they closed the camp for the winter, a city house in the Scandinavian section in Fitchburg. The painting, they felt, held some proof that my grandmother was a Sami and hung out with reindeer. It depicted a few sod houses resembling those earthen-clad igloos I had seen in Point Hope with people dressed in parkas. There was also a lone dog, canoe-like sleds carved out of sections of trees, two or three raised log caches for storing food above ground, and what looked like a child pulling on the reins of a reindeer. The similarities between the painted scene and Point Hope were striking, even though Grammy was born in a more traditional timbered house. My cousin, Holly Anna Jones, recently shared a photo of that house with me. She also has our grandmother's painting hanging over the fireplace mantel in her living room.

* * *

THERE WAS A KNOCK AT THE PARISH HALL DOOR. It was early. I opened it and was greeted by Lily Oktalik holding a pan with two fish, gutted and ready to fry. I thanked her for the breakfast gift and noticed there was already a line at the building's attached shed housing the chemical toilet. I waved to the group and went back inside.

I brought the fish to the kitchen area of the large room where Kate was already preparing breakfast. She smiled when she saw the fish, ready to cook. As the aroma of a meal soon to be eaten moved through the house, it triggered a memory of that breakfast by the lake when I was a kid, the smell of freshly caught fish frying on the stove. I was also beginning to see similarities between the small town where I grew up in Massachusetts and the Arctic village, where I now lived. I saw similarities between Lily and my grandmother, too, a deep caring for others, a generosity of patience in dealing with people.

We ate quietly together at the table as we looked out through the large plate glass window across the tundra to the sea. The horizon that morning was interrupted by the black silhouette of a freighter just offshore, the North Star III, operated by the Bureau of Indian Affairs. It must have arrived during the night. This was going to be a big day for Point Hopers, the arrival of the yearly delivery of food and supplies.

The freighter welcomed an armada of skiffs and umiaks, each small boat sallying out from shore to receive its bounty. Boxes and crates filled with necessary dry goods, canned vegetables, pencils, notebooks, first aid kits, light bulbs, and numerous necessities to sustain life through the approaching dark months were lowered into the waiting boats as they bobbed beside the hull of the waiting ship. Each small vessel shuttled its bounty of winter's supplies back toward land. When they reached the shore, the men onboard tossed the precious cargo, one item at a time, to those waiting there. Then, like a well-organized bucket brigade to stem a raging fire, with every able-bodied person in the village turning out to do their part, they passed the items down long lines to where they'd be stored until needed. Those too small or ailing were there as well, offering encouragement to the others to get the job done.

The day seemed endless as did the task of transporting supplies over water and across tundra, along the gravel paths of the village to safe storage. No one complained about the monotony of their collective endeavor, what I saw were the smiling faces of people hard at work, a communal happiness, a common purpose. We worked until late afternoon and once the job was done, an exhaustion fell over the entire town. People returned to their homes for supper and a well-earned rest as the black freighter sailed south around the spit and out of sight. I made my way back to the parish hall for a meal of canned tomato soup and a grilled cheese sandwich, comfort food after a hard day.

Jabbertown

MY FATHER SPENT HIS SUMMERS WITH HIS TWO SISTERS, mother and father in a house sitting directly on Horseneck Beach on the edge of Buzzard's Bay, just across the Rhode Island State line. The tradition continued with our family, too, until 1954 when Hurricane Carol destroyed all but a few of the houses that lined the beach. How wonderful it was, for both my father and his dad and then me and him, to be able to run from the house right into the surf; to have our family meals at a table surrounded by open windows, curtains rustling in the salt air breezes or playing board games on porch floors until nightfall. Late afternoons, my dad and I used to watch fishing boats returning to Westport from a day out at sea, and when he'd spot a fishing flag announcing a swordfish having been caught, we'd get in the Packard and drive to the harbor, where, once locating the specific boat and pennant, would have swordfish steaks cut fresh by a crew member for that night's supper.

We continued to go to Horseneck Beach every summer, until that big storm, when any remaining houses worthy of salvage were finally moved by barge and transferred to adjoining lots along the

Westport River. We went again, maybe two more times, when the houses had been relocated inland, but it wasn't the same. Gray stained porch boards and repainted weathered siding did little to conceal the extent of damage from the storm or the move to higher ground. Planks creaked and sagged at the slightest touch, just like some of the neighboring guests I had seen coming to this place, the surviving remnants of old New England families; great aunts and widowed wives enduring one more summer's struggle to uphold tradition although their time was running out.

When my father was a child, sometime in the mid to late-1920s, his father took him to Round Hill in nearby South Dartmouth, the estate of Colonel Edward H.R. Green, to see the *Charles W. Morgan*, America's last whaling ship, launched in 1841. Its final voyage was in 1921, when the *Morgan* found safe harbor in Fair Haven, just east of New Bedford, and sat neglected for four years. In 1925, the historic vessel sailed to South Dartmouth where Whaling Enshrined, Inc. began extensive restoration to the ship. Colonel Green was also on the board of Whaling Enshrined, as well as being the major contributor to the restoration. Green had agreed to moor the *Morgan* on the waterfront of his estate and have it open to the public, charging a fee for each visitor as a way to raise money for the restoration. A few former crew members were rehired and brought onboard to share their tales of recent voyages.

My father had told me how he sat on the lap of one of these men, hearing first-hand accounts of their travels. It must have meant something special to him to be taken there by his father, listening to these men share their memories of that quickly fading era. How did my father feel as he moved about the deck of the great ship? The same way I did when he took me to see the *Morgan* in its permanent berth at Mystic Seaport. I walked that same deck with my dad, like he did with his. I've returned many times since on my own, appreciating the ship's splendor, more so now as I get older. On each visit, I'm still in awe as if it's the very first time I climbed aboard, holding my father's hand as we crossed her wooden deck and descended to the quarters below. Now I run my hand along wooden bunks and rails, hand-hewn timber beams and posts trying to relive a connection, find his words, a story, a feeling still trapped in her hull.

His fascination with that ship and the whaling industry stayed with my dad for the rest of his life. On an overcast day in Point Hope I sat around a table in the parish hall's large open room sharing afternoon tea and stories with a few of the singers and musicians I was working with at St. Thomas. They told me about Jabbertown, a commercial whaling outpost, long abandoned and almost forgotten, not far from where we sat. As they told their stories, I couldn't help thinking that my father would have loved to be in this room with us, hearing these tales from an era he was fascinated with and long since passed.

Just to the east and down along the coastline south of the village were the Jabbertown ruins, a ghost town of sorts that once catered to the needs of the whaling industry late in the nineteenth century. Back then, the newly acquired Alaskan territory was governed using a three-pronged approach—the federal government, Christian missions, and commerce. The United States Bureau of Education represented the nation's interest. The bureau had two roles to fulfill: setting up a plan and the means for educating Alaskan Natives and establishing a program to introduce reindeer herding and hunting to the native population. The latter involved transporting tamed herds of reindeer from Siberia across the Bering Strait and enlisting Sami herdsmen to train the Iñupiat. The role of educating Alaska Native children was then delegated by the bureau to various Christian missionaries to carry out the delivery of instruction in remote villages along the coast and rivers. A not-so-subtle two-step process to replace the Iñupiaq way of life by assimilating children into the new *American* culture and convert them to Christianity. With the passing of the 1884 Organic Act, the Episcopal Church had been designated as the official agent to serve the village of Point Hope, establishing its mission, St. Thomas, and building the first school there six years later.

The United States Revenue Cutter Service, an earlier iteration of today's Coast Guard provided some semblance of law and order in the new territory. The Service collected tariffs and navigated the coasts while keeping an eye on the whaling industry's pop-up commercial enclaves, like Jabbertown. Iñupiat laborers assisted visiting vessels as well as traded and bartered for European, Asian, and American goods. The cacophony of languages that routinely invaded these outposts meant very few of the inhabitants as well as shore-leave whalers were able to speak to or understand each other, hence the name Jabbertown. While Iñupiat workers provided services to the commercial whaling crews coming ashore for needed supplies and rest from the long months at sea, they also whaled, not for subsistence as was their tradition, but for profit. The Iñupiat in Jabbertown weren't from the nearby village. The elders, whaling captains and their crews of Point Hope worked together to protect the village's traditions and customs, pushing back against this early Americanization of the region's Alaskan Natives. Trading and commercial relationships with outsiders still took place in Point Hope, but it was entirely separate and distanced from the profiteering that was taking place in Jabbertown.

I wonder if my father, when he was on the deck of the Morgan as a young child, had heard any of the stories that might have chronicled the ship's journeys to this Arctic region. If he did, he never mentioned them to me, and the time to ask him has now long since passed. More recently, I wanted to know if the Morgan had ventured as far north as Jabbertown around the turn of the century. I haven't found any evidence yet, but I did discover in reading through the ship's logs, that Voyage 14, which departed San Francisco in December of 1887, had made its way at least as far as St. Michael's Island in the Bering Sea sometime in May 1888. St. Michael's, like Jabbertown, served as a site for one of the shore whaling encampments patrolled by the U. S. Revenue Cutter Service. To go any farther north once past Nome at that time of the year would have been problematic for the *Morgan* or any other vessel. The Arctic ice pack surrounding Point Hope would have made any attempt at reaching Jabbertown impossible. No one wanted a repeat of the Whaling Disaster of 1871, when thirty-three ships in a fleet of forty were trapped in pack ice off Wainwright and stretching in a line over sixty miles. With ships abandoned, captains and crews journeyed southward some seventy miles in whale boats seeking rescue and safe passage to Honolulu on the remaining seven surviving vessels. Some ships were completely crushed under the pressure of the encroaching drift ice while others were salvaged for wood and supplies by local Iñupiat.

Stories of ships and whaling, those I heard from my father, from Alaskan Native villagers and those uncovered in my quest to learn more about this era, only reinforce my admiration for the people of Point Hope, their desire and need to maintain a culture continuously threatened by the ever rising sea and unrelenting erosion by outsiders like a virus with wave after wave of never ending variants—commercialism, disease, alcoholism, religion, education, land grabs—the list goes on and on.

Bears, Burials, Bubble Gum, and Baleen

A POLAR BEAR ON THE PROWL WALKS into the village and confronts a hunter walking along a path. The hunter stops and realizing he doesn't have his spear or other weapons to fight the polar bear, falls to his knees and begins praying for his life. The polar bear seeing the man with his head bowed low wonders what the man is doing.

"Man, what are you doing on your knees with your head bowed like that?"

The man looks up and now notices that the bear has taken the same position as the man with his head lowered and paws clasped together.

"I'm praying that you won't eat me." The man waits a few moments and then asks the polar bear the same question.

"Bear, and what are you doing with your head bowed and paws together?" The bear raises its enormous head, drool dropping from its tongue, and looks directly at the man.

"Oh, I'm just saying grace."

Lillie Oktalik, the village matriarch and wife of Donald, the Episcopal priest at St. Thomas, broke into a sly semi-toothed grin at the end of her joke. After taking a sip of tea, she stated seriously, "I didn't know that polar bears could talk." Then took another sip, her smile growing even bigger.

We were once again sitting in the parish hall around the table having tea, something that happened regularly at four in the afternoon, a fading vestige of high tea, the custom having been introduced to Point Hope by one of the first Episcopalian missionaries in the late nineteenth century.

A seminary student and his wife, Richard and Kate, were also sharing the parish hall with me that summer. Their bedroom was a small classroom off the larger assembly room. Kate recalled the Fourth of July celebration just a few weeks earlier. The holiday coincided with burials in the whalebone-fenced graveyard out past the landing strip. The snow and frozen tundra prevented digging graves until well after the thaw, which typically meant late June or early July. This year, the burials of those that had died during the fall, winter, and spring when the ground was frozen solid, took place on the morning of Independence Day. Often the deceased, or so I was told, would be stored on the roof of the house of the departed's family until the designated day for burial.

I'd also heard tales of how the elderly, ill, frail and those facing death, would sometimes leave the house in winter, freezing to death or ending their life in some other way. I remember hearing that dying inside among those who shared the dwelling would render the house sacred and would send the family off to find another place to live until the spirit settled. Another story involved the eldest son ceremoniously killing his aging father with a large hunting knife at the father's request.

Over the years I've struggled with this suicidal practice, doubting whether I had heard it correctly at the time. Recently reading Knud Rasmussen's report in the Royal Geographical Journal chronicling his Fifth Thule Expedition (1921-24) along the Northwest Passage and down the northwestern Alaska coast, he states that when an elderly person who feels that he has become a burden to his family due to his age and health will commit suicide, usually by hanging. The practice was not uncommon and often assisted by his relatives.

After burials and services were finished, a line of people could be seen snaking its way back from the Point Hope cemetery to the village, crossing over the permanent imprint of tank tread marks from the 1940s, the airstrip and finally along the crisscrossed paths of the village. Once everyone was back, the Independence Day activities could begin. There were games, songs and races for younger children, teenagers, adults, and the elders, all in categories that matched each group's skill levels and abilities. Kate had packed a few boxes of Bazooka bubble gum before leaving their home in Virginia for Alaska. Each small rectangular piece of gum came individually packaged in a red, white and blue wrapper, a small comic strip was also inserted between the outside wrapper and the gum. Kate had selected a bubble gum chewing contest for the village elders. Sitting together side by side on benches, each person was given a piece of gum. Kate blew a whistle to signal the start of the contest. The elders unwrapped individual pieces of gum and popped them in their mouths. Time seemed to stretch on with no one seeming to show any chewing motions, jaws remained still. Lips and tongues weren't at work forming big, perfect pink bubbles. Kate thought they were too focused on enjoying the flavor. Five minutes went by and still no bubbles. The contest was finally called and Kate, seeking answers to the lack of jaw motion and bubbles, asked the elders to open their mouths. To her surprise she saw that in each person's mouth was a perfect rectangle of Bazooka, then she noticed that very few of the elders participating had full sets of teeth. There was no way with so many gaps they'd be able to chew the gum until it became soft and pliable enough in the allotted time to form a decent bubble. We all had a good laugh as our storytelling session came to an end.

With teatime over, I ventured outside for a walk. I passed Donald Oktalik's house, the rectory, and found him working a chunk of walrus tusk on a board resting on two sawhorses. He appeared to be carving an intricate two-headed walrus about an inch and a half tall. It looked like it could be a small bottle stopper, except holes had been bored using a tiny drill around the base. This intricate carving would become the finial for the lid of a basket. There was another piece of ivory nearby, octagonal, bigger, and flat with similar holes; it seemed to be a companion, something similar in its aesthetic, the creamy color, maybe from the same tusk. This chunk of ivory would become the basket's base. Long strips of baleen, like the flat gimp cord used to weave lanyards, were draped across the sawhorses. These strips were threaded through the tiny holes in the base and finial and woven into a basket and lid. I had only seen a few others before, a couple in a museum in Anchorage and one, extremely expensive, at a small gift shop, *Solveig's on the Steps*, also in the city.

"Donald, what are you making?"

He was always tinkering, whether it was carving something out of bone or wood that could serve a function, like a replacement part for a snow machine. He was his own hardware store. Right now, he was in a state of creative flow when I interrupted him. A moment passed before he looked up and saw me standing there watching him at work.

"Just doing some carving." It was all he said and went back to it. It was his quiet time, so I left him alone.

I continued my walk, passing the spot, where a few days earlier I began collecting wormwood in a plastic bag, thinking of Rimbaud and Verlaine and absinthe. In college once, Herb and I—I often imagined us as a contemporary Rimbaud and Verlaine—finished a bottle of chartreuse thinking we'd get the same reaction as drinking absinthe, it was green after all, but all we got was terribly sick.

I stuffed the bag with the furry-leafed herb with its delicate yellow flowers. I planned to make my own absinthe once back at St. Mary's after I departed Point Hope. When the day came to leave the village, I remember shoving the bag under my seat on top of a dead salmon in the cabin of the plane that would take me to Fairbanks before I headed back to Anchorage. Later, when I did get back, I stored the now decaying plant in the garage at the rectory where it soon turned slimy with mold until, having no choice, I had to throw it out. Alas, no *la fée verte* for me.

I continued my walk toward the shore, something I found very settling, a daily walking meditation watching waves as they met the shoreline then departed, in and out. I adjusted my breathing to match the ebb and flow of the Chukchi Sea as it moved across the gravel beach. As always during my time in Point Hope, the sun continued its daily 360° crawl around me, never quite meeting the sunset-starved horizon.

Departure

O N   A   S U N D A Y   I N   L A T E   A U G U S T ,   T H E   C U L M I N A T I O N   of my
summer's work with the choir and musicians of St. Thomas
was celebrated in the mass I had composed for St. Mary's back in
Anchorage. My time here had been meaningful. I learned more
about myself as a teacher and as a musician, my ability to bring
people together around music, about my status in the village as
an outsider, and what it meant for me to be welcomed into this
community. I still carried a deep feeling of isolation while in Point
Hope and that isolation increased my ability to focus on what I
was sent here to do—to provide musical support and training for
the local singers and musicians. I was doing this work as a conscientious objector, in service to my country, using my knowledge,
skills and talent to make a difference with the people around me.
The hardship associated with being a CO was fading while I was
in Point Hope and replaced with a deep sense of joy and fulfill-
ment. Here I was unhindered by the outside distractions and con-
veniences of city life. There was no place to go, no bookstores to
visit, no coffee shops, diners, or Chilkoot Charlie's to hang out in. I
simply passed the time surrounded on three sides by the Chukchi

Sea, the never-setting sun, and a welcoming community of people. When I think back to my time in Point Hope I experience an hira-eth, a Welsh word which captures my longing for this village that was no longer there, relocated to higher ground a few years later to escape the ever-rising sea level. A homesickness for a place that I may not really want to return to, but still need to know that I had lived there, if only for a brief time.

On that Sunday, however, I knew that winter was coming, the light was changing, and the nights getting colder. High school-age kids were preparing to ship off to boarding schools operated by the Bureau of Indian Affairs in Sitka, Wrangell and the Lower 48, a surviving remnant, barely functioning, of the early nineteenth century Civilization Fund Act. The act strove to *civilize* indigenous young people and assimilate them into American society and customs, as well as convert them to Christianity.

I thought back to my brief stay in Kotzebue on my way to Point Hope and the tense encounter with the three men who confronted me, because they saw me as a white outsider in their village, someone not to be trusted. No one in Point Hope ever made me feel like an outsider, no one called me *gussuk*, or made me feel like a colonizer or missionary. I was not there to convert, nor did I feel complicit in the havoc wreaked upon an indigenous people once Alaska had been discovered by Europeans in 1741. I did, however, begin to realize how the invasion of a Western way of life somehow, for better or for worse, resulted in me being in this village at the edge of the world.

I knew I would be leaving Point Hope soon, but I didn't know the exact time or day or exactly how. There was no agreed-upon end date for my time here and no scheduled flights of any kind to get me out.

After the service, I thanked the members of the choir and musicians who joined in on the mass and who had worked so hard with me during the summer. I spent time straightening up music and hymnals in the church. I enjoyed this time of quiet after a service, a time to reflect on how the music supported the mass and the contribution the singers and musicians had made in setting an appropriate mood for worship. Then I heard the drone of an approaching plane. Leaving the church, I walked out toward the airstrip, joining others as they headed for the runway. Coming in from the south I could make out the shape of a single engine plane cutting across the sky and descending over the tundra as it made its way toward us. I had no idea of who was flying in on a late Sunday morning, but as I moved toward the landing strip, I discovered villagers lining up alongside the runway and waving at the plane as it touched down. They knew it was Bishop Gordon, the head of the Episcopal Diocese of Alaska and beloved former priest at St. Thomas. Bishop Gordon was the man who had asked me to come to Point Hope.

I watched as the Bishop's Cessna 180 six-seater, the Blue Box II, made its descent into Point Hope, wings see-sawing against Arctic winds blowing across the runway. It bounced, once, twice, and then on the third touch of wheels on the runway, it slowed rapidly and made a sharp 180° turn, coming to rest on the side of the gravel landing strip, the engine disengaged. A crowd of villagers surrounded the plane. The bishop emerged from the cockpit and greeted people with open arms. He made his way over to where I was standing with Donald and Lily Oktalik, and the Virginia seminary student and wife. He greeted each of us with a warm embrace. We walked over toward the church and entered the parish hall to prepare lunch in the same space that Bill Gordon had held prayer groups and religious study classes for many years when he served the Point Hope community. Bill checked to see if Richard and Kate were ready to head back to the Lower 48. He asked if I was ready to go also, unless, he said, "You'd like to remain for another month or wait for my next flight into town." I questioned what the weather would be like a month from now and told him I'd be packed and ready to go in thirty minutes. I also had my responsibilities to attend to at St. Mary's now that summer was ending.

Back at the plane, I stowed my guitar and duffle bag, carving out a space in the already cramped cabin. The four of us would fly onto the Athabaskan village of Hughes on the Koyukuk River. We'd be taking on one more passenger, Ted, another CO heading back to Fairbanks. I'd met Ted back in the spring when he came to Anchorage for the diocesan convocation. We corresponded a few times since meeting and he'd sent a few photos of his village, Hughes, where he was doing his alternative service. The pictures were taken during an ice fog and portrayed an eerily bleak scene of village life as seen through suspended ice crystals and filtered sunlight. It would be good to see him again.

I moved toward the rear of the plane, noticing two jump seats. This type of drop-down seating was often found in bush planes to accommodate a small cargo, if necessary, in lieu of passengers. I noticed a haul of bright-eyed salmon and other treasures stowed on the floor beneath the jump seats. The gifts were brought onboard at Bill's previous stop on today's journey. I did my best to avoid stepping on or looking at the fish by tossing a loose canvas tarp over the catch. I then shoved my bag of wormwood on top of the fish and pulled down one of the jump seats and snuggled in for the flight.

As we taxied out to the end of the runway, I thought about flying onto Hughes and then Fairbanks later that day. I also thought about the emergency position-indicating radio beacon and where it was kept on the plane. I was nervous about today's flight. The good thing was that the Cessna 180 Skywagon, an aerial station wagon, was widely respected by Alaskan pilots as a formidable bush plane, extremely reliable. Oh, and having a bishop as the pilot should count for something, even with his sketchy flight record. People often mentioned how Bill had *an angel on his wing*, especially after someone had witnessed the damage caused when his unplanned landings resulted in mishaps.

We took off, circled the village, people below gathered on the landing strip. As we headed east, I took one last look at Point

Hope. I tried to make out people on the ground and was able to pick out Donald and Lily along with new friends I had made during my music sessions and choir rehearsals. They were waving up at us until the plane ascended through low level clouds and I lost sight of them. The abrupt departure gave me little time to say goodbye to everyone I had befriended during my stay. It was like a door slamming shut, a level of unintended rudeness in leaving without offering a warm farewell or saying thanks to those who went out of their way to make me feel like a welcomed member of their community. I thought about my experiences and what I learned while living on this spit of land, shaped like a curved index finger jutting out into the Chukchi Sea. I appreciated the villagers' perseverance, living in these extreme conditions and how hard their lives were. I even grew to eat muktuk without gagging. I had been welcomed into the community, regardless of my otherness or despite the acts of earlier outsiders whose purpose for interacting with this place, like in so many other villages in the Arctic, was often one-sided, with little benefit to the Alaskan Natives. My short-term survival in this place depended on me questioning my biases, fighting off learned stereotypes, and eliminating any air of superiority I may have dragged along from my upbringing. I learned that the Iñupiat lived up to the meaning of their name, *genuine people*. If anyone was superior in this world, it was the people of Point Hope who made this often-inhospitable land their home for thousands of years.

To this day, I consider myself an outsider, always searching for community, the human need to belong. It's a small and quiet voice that still colors my perception of what it means to be included, and where I have brought people together through music and the arts, as a school principal or by leading community acts of dialog and deliberation. I've often felt outside the very groups I've worked with or lived among. For a while I even borrowed these words attributed to William James, placing the phrase on letterhead and business cards, capitalizing on my outsider status until I divined its arrogance: "Only the insights of the outsider will correct the inevitable errors of the insider." Looking back, no other experience has helped shape my worldview as much as my stay in Point Hope, where my isolation as an outsider allowed me to define what it means to be a part of an inclusive community—the realization that true tolerance and acceptance are essential if our neighborhoods, governments, and institutions are to be a safe harbor for all. I had discovered a truth here in this remote Arctic village: we are all tied together, and all life is one.

We made our brief stop in Hughes, its airstrip straddling a bend in the river, easy to overshoot the runway in either direction and end up in the Koyukuk's waters. Villagers brought a few more fish to the plane. Ted, the CO who had been stationed here, walked over to join us carrying his backpack and bulging duffle. I wondered how the additional fish and Ted's stuff would fit in the already crowded cabin. It took a little maneuvering, but we made it work and departed for Fairbanks, a little more than two hundred nautical miles southeast of Hughes. I spent the night in the rectory before heading back to Anchorage the next morning on the Alaska Railroad: a twelve-hour journey. That evening I broke bread with Bishop Gordon and Ted. We shared a barley stew with crusty sourdough bread. Later that night, in our shared bedroom, Ted and I recounted stories of our time spent as conscientious objectors. His alternative service was now finished and tomorrow he'd be flying out of Fairbanks for home.

The next morning, I boarded the train for the journey home. The trip by rail was a real treat. I found a seat in the observation car with its domed glass ceiling offering unrivaled views of Alaska's natural beauty. I ventured to the dining car, grabbed a sandwich, and purchased a beer, my first beer since Kotzebue—Point Hope had decided to be dry rather than having to deal with the damage that alcohol could wreak on a small and isolated Native village—and rejoined my fellow passengers in the elevated luxury of the observation car. Each new vista was announced by the squeal of the rails as wheels met sharp curves and rounded new bends in the track. From valleys to massive mountain peaks, the views were magnificent. When we saw Denali, all talking and laughter ceased. At an awe inspiring 20,310 feet, it was the highlight of the trip back to Anchorage.

Other than a few whistle-stops along the way, our only other interruption on the trip took place when a moose stood on the track and refused to move, even with a blast from the engine's air horns, the animal was reluctant to budge and would leave when he was good and ready, which he did in another twenty minutes or so.

I continued watching the wonder of Alaska through domed windows, the soft chatter of passengers meshed with the rhythmic pulse of the train as wheels percussed over the rail's joints and squats. I fell into a trance listening to that score, a soundtrack to the beauty outside my window.

Then it came to me. There was a presence, there had always been a presence, regardless of what you called it. I no longer had to question it. It spoke to me through sound, through music. It was everywhere and nowhere all at once. I heard it in the Arctic winds blowing across Point Hope, the circling winds around St. Mary's. It whispered to me when playing Bach's French Suite in C Minor or Trois Mouvements Perpetuéls by Francis Poulenc. It filled me when choirs sang, or marching bands played. It lived in folk songs and opera and cakewalks, salsa, reggae, disco, and jazz. The presence haunted bagpipes and drums, pipe organs and ran along the strings of my banjo. It spoke to me through Billie, Duke, Judy, and Liza, every voice and instrument a sacred vessel holding holy harmonic sacraments. The sacred sound in me hears the sacred sound in you. It wasn't about seeing God, it was about hearing God—an unexpected epiphany as the train's tempo slowed and we pulled into the station, our last stop, Anchorage.

Bourbon and Lemonade

IT REGULARLY OCCURRED TO ME DURING MY TWO YEARS in Alaska that no one was keeping me here, no one stood over me to make sure I toed the line. The fact was, my local draft board never checked in on me, I never heard about or saw a form sent to Alaska Children's Services or Chuck Eddy regarding my service, behavior, or work ethic. Perhaps there was one at the end of my two-year stint, but no one ever signed off on anything that I knew of by the time I left. I did receive a letter from Mamie, the board's executive secretary, indicating that my service requirement was met, two months after I'd returned home.

My time as a CO was coming to an end. I had an offer of a teaching position, brokered by Tay Thomas, a St. Mary's parishioner and wife of Alaska state senator, Lowell Thomas, Jr., at one of Anchorage's high schools as part of a hybrid humanities course including social studies, English and the arts. If I wanted to stay in Alaska, there'd be a job for me. I now felt like I belonged here, that I was part of a community that I had been searching for, a feeling in my heart that I belonged. Something unresolved caused me to hesitate, something was calling me home, and I turned down the job. Looking back now, I realized that what was calling me home was the creative chaos of the Northeast, the frenetic energy that kept you edgy and sane at the same time. I had done what I needed to do. In a time of war, I had stood my ground as a conscientious objector and served my time without taking another person's life or losing mine. My mission was complete. Now I just wanted to go home and be with family and friends and reunite with Herbie.

During these last few weeks, Chuck Eddy and I would regularly sit together in the rectory dining room, wooden chairs facing out large picture windows toward the Chugach Mountains. Behind his clerical collar, Chuck was still a Kentucky boy at heart. He'd mix us tall, ice-filled glasses of overly sweetened lemonade topped off with half a glass of bourbon each. Not something I would ever order at Chilkoot Charlie's or anywhere else for that matter, but something I still make to this day when I have the urge to remember. When I do, I'm immediately brought back to that time and place when Chuck and I would sit in late September afternoon silence and watch the clouds sweeping up from the base of the Chugach range, pushed aloft by winds cutting across the valley and coming to rest as if asleep on the tops of mountains.

There was a farewell party planned for the next week. It was to be a surprise, except that someone leaked the plan to me, I think forgetting that I was the one to be surprised. Feeling like such a fuck-up at times over these previous two years, I doubted that I could ever cross that threshold. I didn't want to be recognized or honored. Instead, I sold my car and bought a one-way plane ticket to Chicago, once there, I'd change planes for Cleveland before booking a flight to Allentown. I asked Chuck to drive me to the airport a few days later before the farewell celebration happened. There were no words at parting, just a bear hug goodbye which in my heart, still keeps me warm. I boarded my flight for home leaving Chuck standing at the gate.

* * *

CHUCK DIED AUGUST 9, 2020, A Sunday, just as I finished writing this chapter. I made myself a bourbon and lemonade after hearing the news from my longtime Alaska friend, Mary. As I sipped my drink and typed through tears, I thought about this man who had made such a difference in my life, how he was able to challenge me with projects that he knew would spark my creativity and humanity, helping me become a better man and doing good for others.

Cuyahoga Falls, Ohio

I BOARDED THE NORTHWEST ORIENT 747 IN ANCHORAGE and found what appeared to be an empty plane, except for the cabin crew who remained scarce throughout the redeye flight to Chicago. I could pick out one or two other passengers seated in their own sections. We had all been separated it seemed, either because there was so much room onboard or to keep the three of us from conspiring on ways to request meals and drinks during the long flight when all the crew wanted to do was sleep. For whatever reason, the westbound leg to Asia of this flight always had more passengers onboard as it made its way to Tokyo, but eastbound, only a few people ever seemed to be returning to the Lower 48. For this flight, Anchorage served as a refueling stop rather than a hub for arriving and departing passengers. Once seated I discovered I had the entire section to myself, so much so that I was allowed to stow my duffel in the row in front of me, my guitar and banjo strapped in seats like two oddly shaped passengers in the row behind. I had already shipped my books and other belongings back to Allentown a few days earlier.

In Chicago, I caught a flight to Cleveland. I wanted to see Herbie first, even before venturing home to my parents. He had taken an organist job at a Methodist church in Cuyahoga Falls, no longer working at the Hackley School in Tarrytown. I called him once I deplaned and in thirty minutes Herb pulled up to the curb in his blue Pontiac LeManns convertible. I threw my duffel in the trunk and wedged my banjo and guitar in the backseat, and we headed south toward Akron.

Once we got to Cuyahoga Falls, Herb turned onto Sachet Street and into his driveway. He lived in a converted one-bedroom apartment on the second floor of a house, the landlady occupying the first floor. Herb gave me a quick tour before he had to go to church for the afternoon. It was a simple layout—living room, a kitchen larger than what was needed for the three room plus bathroom set up. Herb showed me the clawfoot tub, no shower, and instructed me to wipe it down after I took a bath. No soap rings please. He pointed to a sponge for that job along with a measuring cup to rinse off any residual soap suds that might remain on my body after bathing. Herb left for work, and I took a hot bath, rinsed off, wiped down the tub as instructed and then rummaged through my duffle for fresh clothes. I paced through the apartment's rooms for the rest of the afternoon, looking out its windows to the crushed stone driveway below, waiting for Herb to return from work, anticipating an intimate evening together.

We spent that night together in Herb's double bed. A regular bed with an ornate oak headboard. I hung my clothes on the footboard's finial. The mattress sat so high off the floor on the frame's spindled legs that I feared I'd fall out if I turned the wrong way in my sleep. I was used to my waterbed which rested like a silicon breast implant flat on the concrete floor in the storage closet under the stairs in St. Mary's.

I wanted to hold him, I needed to hold him, but was reminded that we'd gone through all that before, hashing out the boundaries we'd established for our relationship during our last year of college. He was straight and I was not. He wanted a family one day in the future, and I didn't know what I wanted at that moment other than Herb. I seemed to have pushed that very truth out of my consciousness over the two years I was in Alaska, loneliness and isolation manifesting in my mind a relationship whose imaginary embers would never be rekindled. Not in the romantic sense, no matter how much I'd hoped they would. I was sure his being straight wouldn't matter as soon as we saw each other again. He could overcome that I thought, but of course it did matter what I thought, and he couldn't overcome being straight any more than I could overcome being gay. We were still close, more than mere college chums, but still just friends, nothing more. As I lay in bed that night, wide awake and frustrated, the realization hit me again, as it had in college, that we weren't lovers at all. For two years I had fabricated a reality that, in truth, did not exist. It never existed to begin with. It was another hiraeth, a longing for something that was no longer there. It was clear that Herb and I shared a strong bond between us, a love in fact, something that we still share to this day. It wasn't the kind of love I had manifested in my mind to survive a loneliness that, for me anyway, could only be remedied through an emotional and physical intimacy with another person. So, even though we were sharing the same bed on this one fall night, something that I had wished for and dreamed about for over two years, I would need to go my separate way when I awoke the next morning. The feeling of loneliness and the need for physical intimacy I thought would be remedied by being with Herbie again, didn't happen as I had expected, but rather followed me home to Allentown.

Epilogue

IN A DREAM, JAMES FRANCO IS THE LEADER OF A NEW CULT religion practicing in the countryside on a makeshift stage off a wooded lane where cars park in a field, accessed through a break in a row of trees by the side of the road. I'm his accompanist and watch him from behind a glass window at the back of the platform, as if I'm in a recording booth, yet I can't hear him to know that his closing benediction has been said and that I've missed the cue and it's now time for me to play the postlude. When I see him gesturing for me to begin, I take my place at a beat-up piano, a spinet, only to notice that some of the keys have been removed and replaced with rectangular pieces of plywood nailed in spaces where the ivories and ebonies used to be. I have an almost octave of lower keys that work and only a few higher ones available. I play from a sheet of music but am annoyed that I thump on wood that doesn't depress or connect with a hammer to strike the strings for those notes that are missing. The sheet music is now useless. I'm having to improvise and when out of habit I reach to strike a familiar note that's no longer there, I must somehow incorporate the sounding thud into the piece. I then notice, when one of the plywood sections comes loose and falls away to the floor, that handwritten notes on small scraps of paper are buried underneath where the piece of wood used to be. Each piece of paper is labelled, *Foundations of the Church*. I stop playing and begin to read the notes. I'm surprised that these scribbled scriptures are hidden here, as if it's the safest, holiest place to hold these sacred tenets of faith, this wrecked piano with peeling veneer and missing keys. I wonder where the keys have gone and who may have taken them. I'm left, as always, with more questions than answers. James Franco just stares at me wondering what's gone wrong as car horns blare their disappointment with the service.

* * *

I HAD BEEN HOME FOR ABOUT A MONTH and began looking for teaching jobs, not an easy task as schools were in session and any open positions had been filled back in August. Add to that the fact that music teaching positions were few and far between. If I was lucky, I could maybe hope for a job opening at the semester break in January. My parents wanted me to stay local and find a job in or near Allentown, but for now my teaching certificate was issued in New Jersey and it would take time and maybe additional college course work to add a new teaching credential from Pennsylvania.

I was able to join the cast of *Promises, Promises* mid-production as a chorus member with Allentown's Municipal Opera company, a community theater group I had worked with while a senior in high school. This gave me something to do, a purpose, even for a few weeks, and a chance to rekindle years old friendships and get out of my parents' house in the evenings.

Some friends from college invited me to join them in Manhattan to see *A Little Night Music*. I was excited and looked forward to reuniting with them and especially in being able to see a hit Broadway musical. I hadn't been in a New York theater in more than two years. Once in the city and among my friends, I had difficulty feeling at ease. The neon lights, the horns and traffic, the crowded sidewalks and chaos of the city and anticipation of going to the theater hit me hard. I shut down, talked little, and wanted out of the city as soon as it was possible, to get in my car, drive through the Lincoln Tunnel and head home. It became clear at that moment, that my reentry to life on the East Coast might take some time.

My mother was cooking up a batch of New England clam chowder, her specialty, and something she knew I loved. While she continued stirring the pot, I went out to get the mail. In addition to household bills and flyers addressed to my parents, there was a small brown paper wrapped package for me from Chuck Eddy at Saint Mary's in Anchorage. I brought it over to the kitchen counter and took a seat on a stool. As I unwrapped the paper covering, I notice an envelope inside and opened it. It was a note from Chuck and a little over $200 in cash. The note read that this was the money collected as a gift to me from friends and supporters who would've been at my surprise party if it had taken place and I hadn't left so abruptly. I appreciated the gift, especially in that I didn't have a job but felt somewhat guilty in that I had run out on their gesture of kindness and farewell.

Once I got through the note and read it again aloud to my mother, I turned my attention back to the box that came with Chuck's note. It, too, was wrapped in packing paper, addressed to me at St. Mary's and with a return address of Point Hope and St. Thomas Episcopal Church. I reread Chuck's note to see if he had added any hints as to why I would be receiving this package, but he hadn't. I removed the outside paper, placed the box on the counter, and grabbed a small paring knife to slice open the tape sealing the box closed. As I carefully removed the shredded scraps of paper used to cushion the package's contents on its long journey from the Arctic to Allentown, I discovered a small taupe basket woven out of baleen and topped with a double-headed walrus finial carved out of ivory and the color of dry barley. It was the basket that Donald Oktalik had been working on that late afternoon when I walked past him and asked him what he was doing. There was a note at the bottom of the box that simply read, "Thank you for sharing your gift of music with the people of Point Hope." I couldn't stop the tears from flowing.

* * *

MY LAST CONVERSATION WITH MOM WAS ON A SUNDAY in mid-November three years after Alaska. On the nightstand within her limited reach was a small electric ice crusher she would use to chip cubes to a comfortable size for sucking to quench her thirst, a fifth of *Jack Daniels* to dull her pain, and a bottle of *Sudafed* to cool her overwhelmed lungs—self-prescribed medicines for someone refusing any form of medical attention. She ate nothing else. She talked about how her muscles had atrophied in the last few weeks. She didn't have to tell me, I could plainly see as I helped her to the bathroom, her urine brown and shit yellow.

Once I got her resettled and comfortable in her bed, I made room for myself and sat down beside her. I was single at the time, and she asked me about two boys I had been friendly with in college. While she was less than tolerant of these friendships a few years earlier, she now asked if I was still in touch with them. I told her that Herb, my college roommate and first love, was now married and very straight; and that Ara was either on the West Coast or somewhere in Hawaii. They were no longer part of my immediate circle of friends. With Herb out of the picture, she mentioned Ara again as someone I should look up and reconnect with, that it was important to have someone in your life you care about and who cares about you. I told her that I didn't feel that way toward Ara; he was just a friend at the time and that I didn't sleep with every boy I knew or befriended or brought home the way she sometimes imagined years before. She smiled.

"You've served your country as a CO, which you know both your father and I are proud of you doing, and now you have a wonderful teaching job in Toms River. I don't want you to be lonely, you deserve to have someone special in your life."

"I'm okay Ma, I have friends. It'll happen, I'll find someone soon."

My mother knew about my feeling exiled, isolated, and lonely during my time in Alaska, the darkness of winter and brightness of summer and living at the edge of the Chukchi Sea. She knew it took me time to readjust to life back in the Lower 48. She also was aware that I had recently broken up with a boyfriend, another friend from college, who I was living with and imagined I'd be with forever only to discover he had a convoluted view on what it meant to be a trusting and monogamous partner. When he found me crying on April 30, 1975, when Saigon fell and the war had ended, turned to me and said, "What are you crying for? You were lucky. You did nothing in the war, you found a way out because you were scared."

My mother's desire for me to find someone to be with let me know how much she cared that she wanted me to be happy and to find someone to love and be loved by.

Then, in an awkward confession she recounted an incident while a freshman at Green Mountain College. She had shared some stories about this time in her life when she was a boarder at the Poultney mayor's house, where she did odd chores, shoveling snow and hauling coal for the furnace, to cover her room and board. She talked about walking to classes in the brutal bleakness of the Vermont winter and then went on to tell me about one afternoon following a French class when the female professor asked her to stop by her office to see her. Later, after her classes had ended and before leaving for the day, she climbed the stairway leading to faculty offices. Knocking on the door, she heard her professor call out to her to enter. Once inside the office, the teacher left her desk coming close to her student, my mother. The teacher placed her hand on my mom's shoulder, coming closer still. My mother stepped back and when another advance was offered, she moved back even more until the professor began to chase her around the large desk. There was no sign of help from the empty hallway outside the office door, most students and professors had left for the day. Whether my mother was able to fend off her attacker, or if the struggle led to submission or further encounters, I do not know. Her confession offered no further details into what happened between them. She only stated that she wished she'd been able to explore her sexuality more fully, like me she added. It's been our secret. I've told no one about it until now.

We sat together for a long time in a not uncomfortable silence on that Sunday afternoon. I kissed her goodbye. It was the last time I saw her. My mother died on Thursday. She was 57 years old.

Acknowledgments

W HILE THE JOURNEY TO ALASKA WAS A SOLO ENDEAVOR, the retelling of it has been a collaborative undertaking. I am deeply appreciative of and indebted to the following for their helpful and specific feedback all delivered with kindness: Herb Chamberlain for always being there for me and for preserving the story in the letters I sent him leading up to and throughout my time in Alaska; Mary Wagner LaFever for sharing her passion in folk music and the Poor Wind coffee house at St. Mary's and who first read my fledgling collection of vignettes in 2013; Dick LaFever for making sure I remained respectful to Alaska Natives in my story and who offered up the term *gussuk* to describe how I was seen by the three young men in Kotzebue; Kristyn Kamps, extra-special friend and colleague, for her continued support and patience in listening to my stories over the many years we worked together training teachers in Bismarck and Grand Rapids, Napa and Palm Springs; artist Joan Duff-Bohrer for her artful insights and critiques and encouragement; Holly Anna Jones, my cousin and family genealogy partner, for sharing stories of our grandmother, Anna Marie Jaukkuri Jones; for Ryan Sprott, whose friendship, encouragement and humanity continue to inspire me; Christian Chalifour for bringing clarity to an evening at the Bonfire Lounge; Karol Libbey for being present and compassionate when it was most needed; Lois Jacobson for her support and love regardless of what she discovered about me while reading the story; Gotham Writers Workshop for having the right training at the right time when I became serious about this project; Cullen Thomas, my editor, mentor and confidant, for his knowledge and wisdom in providing me a structure and the deadlines I needed to complete this work; Phil Garrett and his team at Epicenter Press for taking a risk on a first time author and moving this story out to the world; and, Doug Hunter, my husband and steadfast companion for forty years and whose love and patience allowed me the time I needed to write this book.

Permissions and Attributions

DONALD PROFFIT is a former arts educator and school principal and has presented workshops, clinics and original performance pieces in Australia, Belgium, Canada, France, Israel and Italy. His work in Israel as part of an interdisciplinary arts project brought together Israeli, Palestinian and American youth, using the arts as the vehicle for igniting meaningful dialog between the three groups.

CPSIA information can be obtained
at www.ICGtesting.com
Printed in the USA
JSHW030243020323
38335JS00009B/34